TWENTY-SIX LEAD SOLDIERS

Books by Dan Wooding

Junkies Are People Too
Stresspoint
I Thought Terry Dene Was Dead
Exit the Devil (with Trevor Dearing)
Train of Terror (with Mini Loman)
Rick Wakeman, the Caped Crusader
King Squealer (with Maurice O'Mahoney)
Guerrilla for Christ (with Salu Daka Ndebele)
Farewell Leicester Square (with Henry Hollis)
Uganda Holocaust (with Ray Barnett)
Miracles in Sin City (with Howard Cooper)
'Lord, Let Me Give You A Million Dollars' (with Duane Logsdon)
God's Smuggler to China (with Brother David and Sara Bruce)
Prophets of Revolution (with Peter Asael Gonzales)
God's Agent (with Brother Andrew)

TWENTY-SIX
LEAD
SOLDIERS

Dan Wooding

CROSSWAY BOOKS • WESTCHESTER, ILLINOIS
A DIVISION OF GOOD NEWS PUBLISHERS

26 Lead Soldiers. Copyright © 1987 by Open Doors International and Dan Wooding. Published by Crossway Books, a division of Good News Publishers, Westchester, Illinois 60153.

First printing, 1987

Printed in the United States of America

Library of Congress Catalog Card Number

ISBN 0-89107-454-6

This book is dedicated to the millions of unsung heroes that make up the "suffering church". Their suffering has not been in vain.

"Give me twenty-six lead soldiers
and I'll conquer the world."

attributed to KARL MARX
and to BENJAMIN FRANKLIN

Contents

Acknowledgements

I would like to first of all thank my wife Norma, for her unstinting support in my pilgrimage which has taken me from running a drug rehabilitation centre, to working for Billy Graham. Then reporting for two of Britain's largest tabloids and also as a correspondent for America's *National Enquirer*. Norma stood by me at my lowest points and encouraged me when I made my traumatic career change, to work as an undercover reporter for Brother Andrew's ministry, Open Doors.

I would also like to thank my two sons, Andrew and Peter, for supporting me in the move across the "Big Pond" to the United States, to share the story of the "suffering church" with a much wider audience.

I could not, of course, have done any of this without the Christian upbringing of my parents, two pioneer missionaries who showed me what it meant to follow Jesus Christ as a true disciple, whatever the cost. My sister, Ruth, has also been a great friend to me over the years. Thanks, Sis!

Brother Andrew has been a big encouragement and inspiration to me. It was his courageous pioneering of a ministry behind the Iron Curtain that has inspired thousands to follow in his footsteps, myself included. This self-effacing Dutchman brought a new dimension to me in understanding what the church of Jesus Christ is all about.

Finally, I would like to thank all my colleagues in Open Doors for their unstinting support over the years, especially my assistant Brenda Poklacki and Ruth Larssen, who has checked the manuscript time and time again.

Foreword

I have known Dan Wooding for many years and this book tells us much about God's dealings in his life—sometimes with charming simplicity.

Amazing how many people he knows. One day he drove me through London and, passing under a railway bridge, he pointed to a flower-seller and said casually: 'One of the men from the "Great Train Robbery".'

But all that is not so important; of far more value is that he now knows and meets God's children in the suffering church. And that, I truly believe, is how God looks at our lives; how much do we do to get in touch with our brothers and sisters behind the 'curtains'? How much do our lives count for that 'suffering body of Christ'? I must ask myself that question, too, continuously.

To me the value of this book is to show how God guides a young man and trains him in secular work, to make his life count where it is so much needed: for the suffering church.

I therefore strongly recommend this book to a wide public, and my prayer is that you will be turned on to the most important battle that takes place in the world today: the battle for the minds of people, where the soldiers are of lead; twenty-six of them might win that war.

Brother Andrew
Harderwijk, Holland

PROLOGUE

Stabbed in the Back

You cannot hope to bribe (Thank God) the British Journalist.
Considering what the chap will do unbribed, there's no occasion to.

HUMBERT WOLFE

'I'm going to kill you!' The Scotsman's insane eyes scanned my face for several seconds, then he drew deeply on
his cigarette and slowly blew the smoke out, watching as it
snaked upwards towards the grubby ceiling of The Stab in
the Back pub.

I smiled weakly as I stood at the side of the bar and
stammered, 'But why? What have I done to you?'

The Scotsman gulped a double whisky, turned to me
and hissed, 'Because you know where Maurice
O'Mahoney is and he put one of my friends behind bars.'

The O'Mahoney he was referring to was a London
criminal mastermind turned super-grass. A criminal by
the age of ten, he had been involved in nearly every type
of crime known to man, from hijacking lorries and bank
raids to highly professional burglaries and wage snatches.
But when O'Mahoney was caught, he informed on more
than 200 criminals involved in crimes totalling over one

11

and a half million pounds.

Now O'Mahoney was facing life on the run. An under-world contract was out on his life and he lived in constant fear of being tracked down and savagely killed.

I had co-authored a book called *King Squealer* with this criminal who always carried a Magnum whenever we met at a series of secret hideouts. The story was serialized in the *Sunday People,* the tabloid I worked for.

As I tried to stop my whole body from shaking with fear, the hit-man continued, 'There is only one thing that can prevent you from dying tonight . . . you have to tell me where that swine is. If you don't, well I've got a knife in my car outside and I plan to get it and slit your throat.'

My mind raced for a response as his huge, staring eyes bored into my very soul. I knew he was not joking as his reputation had gone before him. My brow was awash with perspiration as he ordered another Scotch from 'Boy George', the large, curly-haired bartender who so enjoyed 'mothering' the many journalists that packed this pub off Fleet Street.

'But,' I responded, as a lump gnawed at my stomach, 'I . . I . . . don't know where O'Mahoney lives. He never told me where I could contact him . . . just in case of a situation like this.'

I tried to catch the eye of another reporter hovering nearby, but he was intent on his conversation with a re-porter from the *Daily Mirror.* I desperately scanned the bar, hoping that someone would help me. Suddenly, one of my colleagues, seeing the look of terror on my face, ambled over.

The Scotsman was not pleased and blew smoke into his face. 'Hey, there's no need to do that,' my fellow scribe protested as he wiped the stinging smoke out of his eyes.

'Anyway, what have you been saying to Dan?'

Before he could answer, I responded, 'He says he will kill me unless I tell him where O'Mahoney is.' With that I heaved myself onto a bar stool and hooked my legs around it.

'Look,' he said, eyeing my potential killer, 'I don't know what your game is, but don't come in here making threats like that. Dan's just doing his job. If you want to get your revenge on the "squealer", that's your business. But don't go behaving like this.'

I could see two heads 'rolling' by the end of the evening, if he continued.

The arguments about whether or not I should die continued for an hour amid the smoky swirl of the executioner's omnipresent cigarette. Drinks were bought and downed and gradually the atmosphere brightened a little.

As he swallowed another double whisky, I ventured, 'I sympathize with your anger over your friend, but please don't take it out on me. Like my friend said, I was just doing my job.'

That was always the excuse we journalists in Fleet Street used when we were involved in some of our shameful escapades. In fact Fleet Street was dubbed 'The Street of Shame'. To many, we were expected to be giants with the pen. After all, weren't we following in the footsteps of William Shakespeare, H.G. Wells and Somerset Maugham? Hadn't we British, ever since Johann Gutenberg's twenty-six soldiers of lead first marched across the pages of history in the mid-fifteenth century, led the way? We 'hacks' on the British tabloids, however, now appeared to the critics to have an insatiable urge to destroy all that was once great in our own country. Now it seemed we were nothing but town-criers publicly proclaiming the misdeeds and misfortunes of the high, mighty, mediocre and detestable.

'But what of our misdeeds?' I had often pondered. 'Who judges us?' Like one prime minister had said of the British press, 'You have power without responsibility.'

Another twenty minutes passed and suddenly, for some inexplicable reason, the granite-faced Scot crumbled and emotionally threw his arms around me.

'Dan, I came here tonight to kill you. Now I really like you.' He fished around in his pocket and produced a ten-pound note and handed it to me.

'Here, have a few drinks on me.'

With that he stumbled out of the bar. I was shaking with emotion. Would he be back? Would he be waiting for me outside the pub with *that* knife?

'That was a close one, Dan.' My friend eyed the money and said, 'I think we need a drink. I reckon we've earned it, don't you?'

My hands were shaking helplessly as I gulped a quick drink. My friend looked at me with unusual compassion. 'You've been having a rough time lately, Dan. Do you want to tell me about it?'

I did. And soon it was as if a cork had been pulled from my subconscious and it all spilled out.

'I came into Fleet Street as a Christian, thinking I could change the world,' I told my colleague. 'I truly believed that I could contribute something really worth while through my writing, but now I find I am getting deeper and deeper into something I can't handle.'

He was already aware that I had been featured in the sensational Old Bailey trial of former Liberal leader John Jeremy Thorpe, who was accused with others of conspiring to kill Norman Scott. Thorpe alone was charged with conspiring with financier David Holmes to kill Scott. Thorpe, who pleaded not guilty to both charges, was later acquitted on all charges. Before the trial began I had been commissioned by a publisher to co-author Scott's autobiography. During the trial the judge had asked to see the contract. When he read my name on it he had uttered the immortal words, *'Who and what is Dan Wooding?'* The statement was faithfully reported in the national press and now my evangelical friends knew that I had agreed to work on a book with Scott. Most were horrified that I would be involved in such a project.

'Well, Dan, let me ask you, "Who and what is Dan Wooding?"' That was like a knife to my heart. For I didn't know any more.

'Did you know that my life has also been threatened by another gangster and just a few weeks back, while I was out of the country, I thought Norma, my wife, had been murdered by an associate of this man.

'Now, this very week, I've been told that our home phone is being tapped because of my underworld reporting. Scotland Yard wants to know what I'm talking about to these guys. Tonight, well, that was the final straw. I didn't think it would ever be like this.'

My colleague looked at me as if I were just a little mad.

'You still haven't got it, have you, Dan? In this game *we are not paid to think.*'

With that he was off. I followed him out into the winter's night. As I walked out into darkened New Fetter Lane, the snow tumbled thickly out of the sky and my heart felt cold.

'God,' I prayed, 'If I'm not paid to *think,* what am I doing here? What has gone wrong with all my good intentions as a Christian? I thought "all things work together for good . . .". I can't see any good thing coming out of my present situation.'

At that moment, I didn't know what my next step should be. All I knew was that I wanted to get home to Norma and my two sons, Andrew and Peter, and enjoy being with decent people again.

I felt I needed a shower to cleanse away the filth of an evening like this.

I

African Odyssey

No pain, no palm; no thorns, no throne; no gall, no glory; no
cross, no crown.

WILLIAM PENN

The shrilling of crickets, the eerie whistling of night birds
and the distant howling of hyenas intruded into the still
night air of the delivery ward of Vom Christian Hospital in
Nigeria. It was just six days before Christmas, 1940, but
there was little goodwill in a world convulsed in the mayhem of World War Two that had begun on Sunday, September 3, 1939, when British Prime Minister Neville
Chamberlain declared we were at war with Germany.

As the former Austrian house painter, Adolf Schickl-
gruber, was trying to take over the world, I was struggling
to get into it. After eight hours, I finally appeared, bawl-
ing and spluttering.

'You've got a boy, Anne,' said Dr Percy Barnden, a
British missionary doctor, as he snipped my umbilical cord
and then slapped a mosquito that was probing his arm. My
mother smiled gently as she looked down at her first child.

My father, Alf, was anxiously waiting in his mud-walled
home in Izom, a remote bush village some 600 miles away,

16

for news of the birth. A telephone call from the hospital, operated by the Sudan United Mission, to the British government outpost in Abuja, announced my birth. Then an African messenger walked thirty miles to Izom to see my father to tell him the good news. He arrived on Friday, December 20.

'You have a son,' beamed the exhausted courier to a background of bleating goats, barking dogs and shouting boys.

A cheer broke out among the many natives, as they crowded into the small Wooding compound. They laughed, danced and clapped their hands. My father smiled, pride showing in his eyes. Now, he knew, would come the traditional naming ritual.

'We must call him "Dan Juma", which means Son of Friday,' said one of the natives, dressed only in a loin cloth.

'Yes,' the others chorused. 'He is to be Dan Juma.'

Much tongue-clacking greeted the new name. The 'resolution' had been unanimously carried, and so my father decided not to tell them that I had, in fact, been born not on Friday, but Thursday. Talking drums quickly spread the news that 'Dan Juma' had arrived.

My father packed a few belongings for the long trip to Vom, which included a twenty-four-hour truck journey to Minna and then a long rail journey to Vom, situated on the Jos Plateau. It was Christmas Eve when we met for the first time. I was a little mite, gurgling with joy, as I looked into the weatherbeaten open face of a courageous little man from Liverpool, who had obeyed God's call and left his home to bring the gospel to a sweltering land where millions had still not heard of Jesus Christ. Where tribe after tribe had been caught in the bonds of animism, witchcraft and ancestral worship, while millions had already turned to Islam.

After a few weeks of rest for myself and my mother, who was also from Liverpool, we eventually returned to the dusty village of Izom, a cluster of mud huts crowned with grass roofs. Many Muslims lived in the community and one of them, an old chief, was soon to provide us with a meal ticket. As I lay in my cot in a temperature of 110 degrees Fahrenheit in the shade, he swept into our hut, and welcomed us. As he grinned, he revealed a few orange-stained teeth that had survived his seventy-three years of life. My father got out a grass mat for him to squat on and then the chief issued an order to my mother.

'White woman,' he gestured grandly, 'I have some more gifts for you and the "little white god". But first I have a request.'

'Yes, chief,' she replied in her soft, Liverpool accent, as she anxiously eyed the bananas, eggs and the four live, struggling chickens his bearers were holding.

'You must bathe him for me.'

My mother knew this little favour would help replenish our dwindling food stocks. He was, for some reason, fascinated to see the 'little white god' cleansed of all the clinging dust of Nigeria.

'You must also give me sweet tea with Carnation milk in it,' he added.

The tea was served, and Mama, the houseboy, a strapping giant, one of my mother's first converts to Christianity in the area, filled a bowl of water and then my mother proceeded to pour a calabash of water over me, time and time again. The chief had come on several occasions to observe this strange ritual (his large collection of children and grandchildren from his three wives were usually unceremoniously dipped in the pale-green waters of the nearby Guarara River). As I was bathed, his face, a dark map of wrinkles, beamed with happiness. The smoky fire cast dancing shadows across the room.

After it was over, he ordered one of his servants to 'prepare the gifts'. He handed them to Mama, who was forced to chase after two of the chickens that had escaped the attentions of the chief's man. After grabbing both squawking creatures, he wrung their scraggy necks.

'Okay,' said the head man to my father, 'now I have given you a gift, you must give me one in return.'

My father fished about in his short baggy trousers and finally found a shilling and handed over the coin to the chief. With that the ceremony of 'appeasing of the child god' was over; all parties bowed, the chief left as quickly as he had arrived, and our eardrums continued to buzz with mosquitoes.

Mama became a crowning jewel to my parents. 'The local witch doctor was so angry with his conversion that he poisoned his food saying that he had taken the "white man's religion",' said my mother. 'But after three attempts, Mama did not die so the witch doctor concluded he must be a god, so he left him alone.

'Mama not only became our cook, but also helped us in evangelism. He would travel with us and carry us across the streams and then go back for the bicycles. He was strong, well-built and fearless.

'Every Monday, he would travel with us and teach the natives. Three boys became Christians under his ministry and built their own church like ours at Izom.'

My parents are small in stature—around five feet nothing. Neither had the advantage of wealthy parents to send them to Bible college—they both had to work to earn the fees for the Bible Training Institute in Glasgow, in my father's case, and for Redcliffe Missionary Training College, London, in my mother's.

The Beatles were at least fifty years away from formation when my parents were born in Liverpool. Neither had known the other before Nigeria, though my father had attended his wife-to-be's farewell service in the Donaldson Street Gospel Hall, in the shadow of Liverpool Football Club's famous ground in Anfield, in 1937.

It had become a tradition for students who planned to go on to the 'mission field' to attend farewell services around the city and then go to Liverpool's Pier Head to wave off those who were leaving on the huge liners. My father was no exception and he waved Anne off as he had done many others.

She had gone to Nigeria with the intention of teaching the blind in Kano and to do medical work there. Their romance blossomed, however, when they later met at the Minna language school of the Sudan Interior Mission, and on September 5, 1939—two days after World War Two broke out—they were married close to the northern walled city of Kano.

Before their marriage, my mother had pioneered a work among the 6,800 blind beggars in Kano, teaching them to read braille and sharing the gospel with them.

But then, on their marriage, my parents began working at Izom in southern Nigeria among the Yamma section of the Gwara tribe. 'These were pagan people, totally different from the Muslims of Kano,' she later told me. My parents said that up until my birth, this had been tough, but the appearance of a white baby changed everything. They were accepted. I would be strapped on a little wooden chair on the front of my father's upright bicycle and we would bump down seemingly endless dusty trails through nine-foot high grass on either side which concealed many dangers—from snakes to quiet, watching monkeys. My father would constantly ring the bike's bell to frighten off the wildlife and would be greeted in return by the racket of exotic birds over his head.

Suddenly, he would arrive in a small dusty village of straw-roofed mud huts, and a babbling crowd of near-naked people would appear. The sound of the noisy, giggling boys mingled with that of barking dogs and bleating goats. For those labouring in the fields, the word would quickly go round that 'the white god is here', and all work would stop. My father would seize the opportunity to preach to the crowds in the Hausa language. He also kept their attention by singing, and sometimes playing a 10-

inch mouth organ and finally unstrapping a large wind-up phonograph and playing Hausa hymns on unwieldy 78 rpm records. The crowds would literally fight to put an ear close to the large horn out of which blared this 'strange' music.

While my father was away, my mother would open the dispensary for the patients sitting under a large mango tree in front of our rectangular hut, and try to deal with the many medical problems of the area. Although she had only basic medical training, she was still expected to handle many difficult cases, and even at times was called to amputate gangrenous toes with kitchen scissors.

'As the crowds lined up for treatment, Mama would preach to them,' my mother explained. 'He would tell them about the love of Jesus and would often lead them in the singing of choruses. Even after being treated, the people didn't want to leave. They enjoyed the time so much.'

Nigeria was, at that time in 1941, still very much a British colony. But this was an area where not too many pith-helmeted civil servants and missionaries had previously ventured. It was a little too far from 'civilization' to cope with.

But to my parents, it was heaven. My father, especially, had blossomed as he had never done when he lived in the back-to-back terraced house in Liverpool's crumbling Toxteth district. In Izom he was 'somebody'. In fact, he became an unofficial 'judge' and was regularly called upon to adjudicate difficult disputes between natives.

'I would sit under the mango tree with most of the village for company and listen to the arguments,' he recalled. 'Then I would ask the Lord to give me Solomon's wisdom in giving the right judgement or advice.'

'They called me *Mai hankuri,* which means "the patient one".'

As my father dispensed advice and justice, the crowds squatted silently in a semi-circle and I would gurgle con-

tentedly in a swing-chair attached to the mango tree as
Jumpa, my African playmate, pulled the rope to keep me
moving so as to protect me from the snakes and mosquitoes. For my parents, the slithering snakes, monster
rats, bitter-tasting quinine tablets, the tsetse flies constantly humming around their faces, the debilitating hu-
midity, the hot air that clutched at them like a sauna, the
inconvenience of having to constantly boil and filter the
water, didn't affect their unquestioning belief that God
had called them to this remote area of West Africa.

My mother, a small but tough outspoken woman made
of tempered steel, would regularly do battle with the local
witch doctors who dispensed their evil magic. She had no
qualms in approaching them about practising their *juju*
medicine on her patients—something that was illegal
under British colonial law. She had been called in several
times by natives to try and save the lives of people who
had been nearly killed off by the evil black magic of the
witch doctors.

There were even occasions when my parents would be
called to dig up newly-born babies, who had been buried
alive by the superstitious natives because the mothers had
died in childbirth. The witch doctors had told the people
that the evil spirit of the infant had caused the death of the
mother and so the baby had to die, too.

Mama and Baba (the houseboy) would watch in horror
from behind a clump of bushes for a burial to take place.
They would hear the high-pitched shrieking of mourners,
and watch the stiff, white-wrapped body of the dead
mother being lowered into a freshly-dug hole. Then the
usually-crying child, wrapped in a grass mat, was placed
beside her, and the hole filled in.

'When all was clear, they would call us to dig up the
suffocating child,' said my mother. 'If the mite was still
alive, and most were, we would nurse them and then take
them to the mission station at Diko which was run by
fellow-missionary, Esther Anderson. There they had a

large mission church and Christian women would foster the babies under the guidance of Esther. When they got older, these children who had been saved would be sent to a Christian orphanage and many of these babies became nurses and evangelists.'

She added: 'Despite the difficulties, the peace we experienced at the time was indescribable.'

Sadly, the happiness was soon to be broken. It began one night when Alf, my father, normally in bed by 8.30, had not arrived home by 9.30. My mother, by the meagre light of a storm lamp, was painting scrolls containing Scripture verses and choruses in the Hausa language. Just a stone's throw away my mother could hear the ugly sounds of jackals and hyenas quarrelling. She began to worry. Then she heard a rustle outside, and he staggered in.

'I don't feel . . . .'

His words trailed off and he crashed head first onto the floor. He lay there, shaking, his face contorted in pain. My mother knelt down and took his temperature—it was 103 degrees Fahrenheit. Instinctively she rushed to the dispensary for medicine.

In agony, he rolled from side to side, his pain-lined face streaming with sweat. His brown, curly hair, usually immaculately groomed, was lank and damp. He gazed up at his wife with unseeing eyes. At first my mother recoiled in ill-concealed horror. But then she dragged him across the floor, lifted his pain-racked body onto the bed, and covered him with a mosquito net. She gave him medicine but he couldn't keep it down. He lay in the pale flickering half-light, breathing harshly. His lips were pale.

What should she do? Her medical knowledge was minimal and they were eighty miles from the nearest hospital. Dropping to her knees in desperation, she cried in a voice barely audible, 'Lord, I can't cope. Please help, please . . . .' Her face was frozen with tension. But suddenly her mind became clear and she took a stick and a storm lamp and ventured through the dangerous bush to the nearest village and called Ungalu, the house boy, to fetch Mama and ask him to travel to Abuja with a message to the District Commissioner.

Before Mama left on his desperate mission, he came and prayed for my father. As he looked down at his pale face, Mama cried out, 'Lord, he that thou lovest is sick.'

Then it was discovered that the bicycle he was to travel on had a puncture and my mother had to mend this before Mama could set off.

Soon a truck was sent and my mother put in the back of it some folding chairs, a camp bed, a cot basket for me, and food for us all on the long journey to the hospital at Minna. Along the way, the truck was forced to stop at a broken bridge which had to be rebuilt before we could continue. But finally we made it.

So began the drama which resulted in my father's hospitalization. The doctor discovered that he had the usually lethal combination of malaria, liver disorder and dysentery. The staff at Minna Hospital worked hard to save his life, and after a week of treatment, Alf began to claw his way back to waking reality; to regain his strength, his very life even.

Soon he returned to us at Izom and was gradually eased back into his routine as a missionary—visiting local tribespeople, taking Bible studies, and all the duties attached to mission work. For a few weeks he felt fine. Then the malaria returned. It was again followed by liver disorder and dysentery. Esther Anderson treated him at nearby Diko. The cruel tropics were exacting a terrible toll on him, but manfully he struggled on, his emaciated features and yellow skin all pointing to the inevitable fact that Nigeria was no place for him.

Both had served five years in Nigeria and the time had come for a year's rest. Though what awaited them in war-ravaged Britain no one could tell.

2

All at Sea

We shall fight on the seas and oceans . . . we shall never
surrender.

WINSTON CHURCHILL

Tears welled up in my parents' eyes as scores of their
African 'flock' gathered outside the compound to say
good-bye to us. As we got into the back of the open truck,
with our lives packed, lock, stock and barrel into boxes,
the people held hands and sang, 'God be with you till we
meet again.'

My father remembered the scene well. 'The converts
ran alongside the truck for at least a mile, waving and
saying "return soon". The tears just kept flowing from
them and us. It was the most moving experience of my
life. We really loved those people. We all kept waving
until they disappeared in a haze of dust that whirled behind the truck.'

After a long journey to the dockside at Lagos, there
came a dire warning from a khaki-clad British civil
servant.

'Mrs Wooding,' said the grim-faced official, 'you may
not make it to England. Boats are being sunk by the Ger-

mans all the time. You are taking your lives in your hands by making this trip. Do you understand this?'

My mother held me close to her (by now I was a lively eighteen months) and nodded. 'I have the choice of either my husband dying here, or of possibly making it to England and getting proper medical treatment for him. He won't last more than another few weeks here anyway. So I have no choice.'

With that she carried me up the gang-plank of the Dutch passenger ship, Stuvescent, and was guided to our cabin by a steward. My father clutched a battered suitcase as he struggled manfully along behind us. A large trunk and several boxes containing our belongings were loaded in the hold by porters.

'There are ninety civilian passengers on the ship and the rest are soldiers,' announced our Cockney steward. 'We are to be part of a convoy of twenty-eight ships protected by four Royal Navy corvettes. It's going to take a blinking miracle if we all make it back to good old Blighty.'

After he left, my parents in the solitude of the cabin knelt down and asked for that miracle.

'Please God,' my father implored, 'May we all make it safely to England. We hand our lives and that of our baby to you. We are completely in your hands.'

The sirens sent a chill of horror through most of those on board. My father was about to start a funeral service which the captain had asked him to perform for an African passenger who had died of blackwater fever. We were just a couple of weeks at sea when the first German attack on our boat came. Everyone had been instructed about what to do if we were hit.

'Get on the top deck. Cut the rope from a lifeboat and take your children, but be prepared to jump into the water,' said the weary captain, his voice shrill and strident.

'Why do we have to jump?' one woman, with two children clinging in fear to her skirt, asked in a desperate tone.

'Because, madam, you will have just one minute to get off the ship,' he said. He paused then with acute embarrassment added, 'We haven't got enough lifeboats to go round. Most of us will have to end up in the sea.'

My mother quickly harnessed me into a tiny life-jacket and then strapped hers around her body. My father also slipped into his life-jacket. For all ninety civilian passengers on our deck there was just one lifeboat. A member of the crew stood poised with a knife in his hand ready to cut the rope that held that solitary boat. Who got in it was to be anybody's guess. It was going to be everyone for himself.

A huge explosion suddenly rocked the whole ship. Then came another and another. It had been as sudden as a cyclone appearing from a clear blue sky. Smoke began billowing from a vessel to the left and also from one in front. Distant screaming filtered through the smoke as hundreds of people leaped desperately from their stricken ships into the heaving Atlantic. There was utter pandemonium.

'Scatter! scatter!' an urgent voice bellowed from the loudspeaker system. We did scatter—like frightened sheep before a storm. Ships took off in different directions as the Royal Navy escort began the impossible task of fighting off the enemy and trying to rescue survivors from the angry sea. Hundreds drowned in a few minutes.

Our ship shot off with another vessel and after four hours of apocalyptic horror, the captain sounded the 'all clear' and announced that the Germans had retreated 'for the time being' and we could all go to the dining room where a meal would be provided.

All through this I had been oblivious of the danger and was happily running around the deck and through the corridors.

That night brought another order. 'Ladies and gentlemen,' said the harassed purser, his face bleak, 'it is not safe for any of you to sleep in your cabins tonight. I want all the men to sleep in one of the salons and the women and children in another.'

My father went to the purser. 'Sir,' he said in a low voice, 'I know you will think that I am crazy, but I have committed this journey into the Lord's hands and I wish for myself and my family to sleep in the cabin.'

The man looked in disbelief at the frail figure in front of him, and after a few moments of eye-to-eye duelling, said, 'Do you realize that if we are hit, you will not have a chance?'

My father nodded. 'Yes, I know that. But I also know that we are in God's hands.'

As panic-stricken passengers tried to stave off the fear of death with large quantities of booze, the three of us slept soundly that night.

Next morning, a deputation of passengers came to my father with a request. 'Mr Wooding, please hold an informal service for us.' He did this for the remainder of the hazardous journey and daily the room was packed to the doors.

For six nerve-racking weeks our convoy of two zigzagged its way from danger. Each morning passengers would rush to the deck to see if our companion ship was still there. Mercifully, it was. Normally the journey from Lagos to Liverpool took only fourteen days. This epic journey meant forty-two days.

I was, however, quite unaware of the dangers afloat. I would spend hours in the barber's shop sitting on the swivel chair turning around and around. Then the soldiers would take me to the lower deck where they kept the monkeys they were taking back to Britain, and I would laugh at them as they ran around on their leashes.

The sight of the towering Liver Building peeking out through the industrial haze of Liverpool's Pier Head brought a huge cheer from those on board the two ships.

My mother held me close and shouted excitedly, 'Danny boy, we're home at last. Thank God, we're home!'

My father's eyes were brimming. He stood quietly thinking of how five years previously he had set sail to Nigeria, with such high hopes, from this very spot. Now he had returned, a physical wreck—though still alive, just!

We moved into a pebble-dash, semi-detached house in Okehampton Road, Childwall—a pleasant Liverpool suburb—to live with my mother's father Sam, and her sister Ethel. My grandfather, who sported a fine white beard, had been, for thirty years, in both the Royal and Merchant Navy and captivated me with his tales of the sea. I can recall sitting on his lap and listening to endless stories that were as salty as his personality.

Gradually, my father's health improved. He had regular medical treatment at the Hospital for Tropical Diseases in Liverpool and in September, 1943, my sister Ruth was born.

After just one year at home, the SIM decided we should return to Nigeria. 'But there were no ships available as D-Day was being planned and only troops and men urgently needed for the war effort were allowed to travel,' recalled my mother. 'They said, however, that Alf could go, but not the rest of us. I was naturally worried as he was still not too well and I wasn't sure he could look after himself in the tropics.'

So this 'soldier for the Lord' sailed back on a troopship, slept in a hammock, and lined up for 'grub' just like the other 'fighting men' on board.

Back in Nigeria, he felt the all-enveloping peace he had first experienced in the early days of his first term. He moved back to Izom to an ecstatic welcome from the natives there. Then after a short stay he moved on to Zaminaka. While there an epidemic of meningitis swept through the area killing hundreds of people. My father was seconded by the British Administration to travel among the natives handing out tablets to try and fight the illness. As he travelled around the primitive villages he was bitten again and again by the tsetse fly and soon went down with sleeping sickness. That was followed by malaria and then dysentery. He began to shiver, sweat and vomit. Then he experienced terrible headaches, extreme diarrhoea and a discharge of blood. He felt completely frustrated.

'Why, Lord' he questioned desperately, 'should my missionary future be wrecked by all this illness?' There was pathetic misery in his voice.

He was treated by a missionary doctor who became more and more disturbed by his lack of physical progress. 'Why? Why? Why?' my father kept asking the Lord. After more treatment, the attacks just continued and a bitter resentment began to seep into him.

This was compounded when the doctor, peering up from my father's medical records over his half-glasses, told him, 'Mr Wooding, you have no alternative but to leave the tropics—for good. I'm terribly sorry.'

My mother cried a lot in those days. And she became more and more concerned with each letter she received from him. His spidery handwriting had become very difficult to decipher and she guessed the worst. He must be seriously ill again.

One day she got the news she had been dreading. It came from another missionary staying in Liverpool.

'Anne,' she said, her voice hushed, 'I think you should prepare yourself for the fact that you will probably never see Alf again. We've had word that he's near to death. I am so sorry.

'Some 800 missionaries in Nigeria,' she continued, 'have joined in a prayer vigil for Alf. But things look hopeless.'

Arrangements were made to put Ruth and myself into a home outside of Manchester, while my mother caught the first available ship back to Africa in the hope of seeing him one last time before he died.

Just two days before she was due to leave, a knock came on the door. It was a telegram from an SIM leader in Nigeria, which said, 'Don't sail. We have put him on a ship to England. It's the only hope.'

Looking like a victim of Belsen, my father finally arrived back in Liverpool and went to Okehampton Road to find that my mother and I were at church. As he walked through the door, Ruth was terrified of him. She ran in fear to her grandfather, wondering who this skeletal figure was.

I can recall returning home and seeing this broken figure standing there, his hands outstretched for love. I ran to him and he swept me up in his arms.

This return journey had not been as dangerous as the last. The big danger to him now was his terrible health. He was, as one doctor described him, a 'museum of tropical diseases'.

Gradually Ruth and I began to accept this little man and learned to love him and give him the affection he so needed after such a traumatic experience.

It was back to the Hospital for Tropical Diseases for him, and a period of heart-searching about what had gone wrong. He would spend two weeks in a hospital and then two at home. That went on for twelve long months. But then the hospital told him he was cleared of sleeping sickness and plans were again put in motion for our return to Africa.

Just as he was getting his life back together, another grievous blow greeted him. A cable arrived from Dr Percy Barnden, the doctor who brought me into the world, saying it would be 'suicide' for my father to go back.

The African odyssey was over, and he knew it. He would have to find a new job.

3

Birmingham Blues

The dispensing of injustice is always in the right hands.

STANISLAUS LEC

The furniture van bumped relentlessly southwards with its sparse cargo of broken-down furniture and the three of us on board. Our destination was Birmingham. It was to be the start of a new life. As the ninety-mile journey progressed through smoke-caked towns like Crewe, Stafford and Wolverhampton, my mother led us in the singing of Hausa choruses. By now we knew a whole selection by heart. Our voices rose as we passed by factory smokestacks spewing black plumes into the air.

My father had already spent three months in this bomb-flattened city working with John Wolf, a Hebrew Christian who had established a missionary work to the city's large Jewish population. Dad had been accepted to work with 'God's chosen people' by the Barbican Mission to the Jews (now called Christian Witness to Israel). Mr Wolf was to move on to another part of the city, so my father was 'chosen' to continue this work.

'I'll find somewhere nice for us to live,' he had confidently told us as we had waved him off in Liverpool.

32

'When I've got that place, you can come and join me.'

Now in July 1946 we had received the good news that he had secured accommodation and our spirits were sky-high.

'I wonder what my bedroom will be like,' I mused aloud.

'Will we have a nice garden, Mummy?' asked Ruth, who by now sported a fine head of light brown curls.

The large green furniture van weaved its way through Birmingham's Bull Ring shopping centre. I pointed to the colourful stalls lining the steep cobbled hill that led precariously down from the Bull Ring into Digbeth.

As we drove towards the south of Birmingham I noticed, even as a child, that the city bore terrible scars of war. Everywhere I saw scenes of devastation. Whole streets lay in ruins. Factories which had once been great were reduced to rubble and twisted metal. World War Two was now well over, but its black scars were there for all to see. Many of the survivors of the 2,241 killed in the bombing would never recover from the mental scars of Hitler's Luftwaffe blitz.

Although large portions of Birmingham had been obliterated by the constant bombing, the area we were now in, Balsall Heath, seemed even more run-down and depressing than others we had passed through.

My mother looked at me and held my hand tight. She seemed bitterly disappointed.

'Brighton Road, Balsall Heath. Is that where we have to go to?' the driver asked my mother as we all huddled together in the front seat of the van.

'Yes, that's right; it's number ten.' She squinted at the letter my father had sent which had the address on it.

I could see that the cloth-capped driver was just as taken aback as we were as he drew up outside a large and extremely drab house which loomed over us like a huge, ugly face.

My mother, with a sick, sinking feeling rising in her

stomach, went and knocked at the front door. A woman soon emerged with a cigarette hanging limply from her lips, and sporting a mass of plastic curlers.

'I've got no rooms to let at the moment,' she barked, 'You'd better clear off.'

'No, I'm Mrs Wooding. I understand my husband has arranged accommodation for us.'

'Oh, that's right.' She flicked ash on the doorstep. 'You've got the attic and another room. You'll have to share the bathroom with someone else though.'

Mrs Reid, a war widow, explained that Mr Wooding had gone out for the day with Mr Wolf on a Sunday school outing to Weston-super-Mare. It was by now late afternoon, and she expected him back at any moment.

'I think you should all come in and have a cup of tea, and then I'll show you your rooms,' she said magnanimously.

We all trooped into her ground-floor lounge and were introduced to Mr Mohammed. His thin lips were pulled into a smile that lit up his swarthy face, showing very small, very yellow teeth.

'He's my special lodger,' she explained, exchanging a grin with her greasy friend. 'He helps keep my spirits up in these terrible times.'

The tea arrived and as we sipped the revolting liquid my father turned up with Mr Wolf, a dark-skinned man. Obviously flustered, he was full of apologies for being late.

First Mr Wolf patted me on the head, then he suddenly lunged at me. 'Now, little Danny, I want to kiss you on the cheek.' His eyes narrowed. I recoiled in fright. Who was this strange figure bending over me? And what was all this kissing business?

'Why should I let you kiss me?' I was defiant.

'Because I want you one day to tell your grandchildren that you have been kissed by a wolf . . . .' With that he kissed me on the cheek and threw back his head and roared with laughter.

As we made our way up the uncarpeted stairs that ascended into shadows, I could see my mother and father exchanging words.

'I'm sorry, Anne,' I heard him say, 'but I have tramped the streets for weeks trying to get something and this is the only place I could find that would take children. Things are dreadful here. There is just no accommodation for couples with families.'

On his meagre wage of three pounds a week, he had found life in post-war Birmingham tough beyond words. Whole areas had been wiped out by Hitler's incessant bombing raids. In sheer desperation, he had finally settled for this seedy house in Birmingham's 'red light' district.

My mother looked in horror at the state of our accommodation as the smell of decay and rot reached her nostrils.

'Alf,' she exploded, 'The place doesn't even have electricity. It isn't fit for an animal, let alone a family.'

In the main 'living room' bugs scuttled up and down the mildewed wallpaper while a few cockroaches fled across the floor, bare of carpet. A dank piece of flowered lino that had probably been in the same place for twenty years, was all that lay between the floorboards and our shoes.

Aesthetics had a low priority in our new home.

'I'm sorry, Anne, but it's the best I could get.' My father couldn't be 'sorry' enough.

Mother fought back the tears of anger as she discovered the dingy place didn't even have a cooker; the shared bathroom was appalling, and the bedroom that Ruth and I were to share was an attic with a gaping hole in the ceiling.

'Come on, Mrs Wooding. It's not all bad,' said Mrs Reid brightly, as she discharged more ash onto the floor. 'There is one problem, however. We have only one gas meter for the whole house. You'd probably be better off using candles.'

She paused to take another puff on her cigarette and allowed it to curl into the recesses of her lungs before continuing. 'The rent is very reasonable. Only twenty-seven shillings a week.'

'But that will hardly leave us enough to live on,' my mother protested.

The landlady's mouth twitched.

'Take it or leave it, Mrs Wooding.'

Mrs Reid was certainly a venomous creature who could turn and sting at the slightest provocation.

On that first night Ruth and I couldn't sleep. The noise of slurred singing from the pub across the road wafted through our window. Suddenly there came the urgent ringing of a police siren. It got louder and louder and was followed by a squeal of brakes.

'It's the cops,' I yelled excitedly as Ruth lay cowering under the blankets.

'Let's have a look and see what's happening!'

I pressed my nose to the dirty window pane and saw in the dim glow of the moon and nearby streetlight two women fighting with each other outside the pub. A group of policemen were vainly trying to separate them as they flailed away at each other. Without warning, the spitting combatants suddenly turned on the police and attacked them. Helmets flew as the men tried to stem the scratching tide of hate.

Things got worse when the pub doors shot open and out poured a group of male drinkers who had decided to come to the aid of the women.

'Come on, Ruth,' I said hoarsely. 'Don't be a scare-baby. Come and watch this. It's really exciting.'

By now she was sobbing in sheer terror. She put her hands tightly over her ears, then hid her face under the pillow.

'It's getting better. There are more police running down the road. Look, there's a Black Maria coming as well. There's about twenty people fighting with the police, but they're winning and pushing them into the van.'

Finally her innocent blue eyes peeked out at mine and

we almost got the giggles.

For nearly three-and-a-half years those nightly fights inside and outside of the Malt Shovel kept me glued to that attic window. It became such a regular occurrence that I didn't wait for the police to arrive. I knew that as soon as 'chucking out' time came, trouble was on its way.

To try and keep our minds off violence, my parents arranged for Ruth and myself to take piano lessons with the mission pianist, Mrs Helen Price, and also to attend missionary rallies at Tennessee, a huge house in the Moseley district, hosted by Mrs Helen Alexander-Dixon, the founder of the Pocket Testament League. These were times of contrast for us both.

When my mother got over the initial shock of her new home, she discovered that most of the residents of the house were involved in a variety of criminal activities. Many had false names because they were on the run from the police.

'At first I found Birmingham more difficult to cope with than Nigeria,' my mother told me. 'The natives in Africa were far more responsive to the gospel and really seemed to love us.

'Mind you, the "Brummies" had just been through a terrible war and life was hard. That included the rationing of food and clothing. It was a struggle for everyone to keep body and soul together.'

Besides trying to find rooms for us, my father had been busy starting up a youth club in a nearby school. It was being attended by some 160 children. He also had a thriving Sunday school there, and had established, with Mr Wolf, a little Sunday night church service in a rented hall.

Our dreadful accommodation was a constant source of embarrassment to my mother, who was used to better things.

'What made things worse was the fact that the police often stood across the road from the house and took note of everyone who came in and out,' she recalled.

'Your father had by now been ordained as a pastor and wore a dog collar. They probably thought he was a bogus priest or something.

'One day my father and sister Ethel came from Liverpool to stay with us. As they went up the steps, the officers ran across the road and stopped them. They questioned them for several minutes about their reasons for visiting the house. They obviously felt they were up to no good.

'Afterwards, my father said, "Anne, why are you living in such a dump?"

'What could I say to him, except, "This is where God has placed us as a family."'

I could tell my father was excited.

'It looks like we've got our own mission hall,' he beamed.

'Well, Alf, that's wonderful,' enthused my mother.

'It seems,' he continued, hardly able to contain his excitement, 'the minister of the Sparkbrook Mission in Alfred Street has to leave Birmingham. His wife is ill and needs to move to a better climate. He wants us to take over the place.' At last he had his own church.

And soon we had our new home. My parents had almost given up hope of ever buying a house for themselves. Through her work serving at a cafe, my mother had managed to save up the huge amount of £200 and hoped that this would be enough for a deposit on a house. But when she enquired about a mortgage, the people at the Building Society laughed in her face and said she hadn't a hope.

'All we can do is pray,' she said firmly. And she did! Every night she would ask the Lord to take us away from those depressing rooms and let us have a proper home of our own.

One day she returned home late beaming with joy. During the summer she often didn't finish until 9.30 p.m.

'Danny, Ruth, Alf, you will be pleased to know that we

have, at last, a new home.' She stopped to wipe away the tears of joy from her face.

'It's a nice area, kids, and the house even has a garden you can play in.' Heaven had finally arrived for us!

4
Your Dreams Can Come True

Whether you believe you can do a thing or not, you are right.
HENRY FORD

My fingers quivered as I counted the morning collection at the back of my father's little wooden mission hall. When I was convinced no one was watching. I grabbed two half-crowns from the collection plate and dropped them into my pocket.

At last I had enough money to get me into the St Andrew's soccer ground for at least the next couple of home games. Birmingham City Football Club had never been as glamorous as their cross-town rivals, Aston Villa, but to me they were everything. I was prepared to lie, cheat and even steal to support them. If I ever missed a home game, my withdrawal symptoms were painful beyond belief.

As I was congratulating myself that morning on my nifty finger work, my father came over to me.

'Oh, hello, Dad,' I said casually, hoping he hadn't seen anything. 'It's been a good offering this morning. Nearly two pounds.'

'That's funny,' he said, adjusting his tight dog collar

40

that seemed to be choking him. 'I would have thought there would have been much more than that.'

'No, Dad,' I lied as convincingly as I could, 'that's all there was.'

When he returned to his flock, I rubbed my sweating palms together, then felt into my pocket and jingled the two coins that were once again going to be my passport to enter the Small Heath ground to see my idol, goalkeeper Gil Merrick.

I had become a City addict after we had moved to our new house in Featherstone Road, Kings Heath, a middle-class suburb on the southern extremities of Birmingham. But my cash-flow problem was not my only difficulty in those days. The other was my parents' opposition to anything they considered 'worldly'. That included the cinema, rock and roll music, and going to soccer grounds. It seemed to me at that time that their motto was, 'You name it—we're against it.'

'Look, son,' my father said one day, 'We are not trying to be spoil-sports, but we just don't think a nice Christian boy should be visiting such places. For instance people gamble on soccer games and we don't agree with that.'

'But,' I desperately pointed out, 'The Blues started as a church team.'

'I don't want any more arguments. You are just not going, and that's it!'

With a streak of independence that I had gained from my mother, I decided that their decision was not final and I would go to St Andrew's anyway. To save further arguments, however, I would carefully cover my tracks so, hopefully, they wouldn't find out.

Each home game, I had another story made up for why I needed to be out all of Saturday afternoon. Standing on the Coventry Road terraces at the west side of the ground on a misty, damp winter's Saturday afternoon, was my idea of heaven. I would shout, scream, and join in the singing of the Blues' anthem, 'Keep right on to the end of the road,' with the other fanatical supporters.

I lived, breathed and dreamed about soccer. When at school we were asked to do creative writing about anything we were interested in, I would write about soccer.

'Wooding, you're quite a wordsmith,' a teacher at Queensbridge School, Moseley, told me one day. 'Have you ever thought of becoming a journalist?'

I shook my head. 'I don't think I'll ever get the right academic qualifications to do something like that, sir.'

The only subjects I was any good at were creative writing and sport.

'Wooding, don't ever say 'don't' again. If you believe you can become a journalist, you can!'

'Yes, sir,' I responded sheepishly, not really believing a word of it.

However, I did begin to write at a more feverish rate. They were usually short stories in which I was the hero . . . . I would save a penalty shot for the England soccer team against the Hungarians in the last minute of the World Cup final, or score a century for England's cricket team against Australia in a Test Match at Lords.

I also began writing a stream of tongue-in-cheek letters to different periodicals. These 'readers' letters' were usually completely fictitious.

One I penned as a teenager under the pseudonym of 'City Gent' caused something of a storm after it was published in the *Birmingham Evening Mail*. It read:

> After living in London for six years I have returned to my native Birmingham and am shocked by the drabness of dress displayed by the average Birmingham male.
>
> Unfortunately, in Birmingham the businessman, when adorned with his bowler, pin-striped trousers and rolled umbrella, is looked upon as a freak. In London the average city man would feel lost without his battle dress.
>
> Please, Birmingham, let us adopt the smart wear of the Londoner and revolt against the cheap, ugly American-style clothes of today.

One irate reader, 'G.E. Jones of Solihull', retorted: 'I entirely disagree with 'City Gent', who wants to put us back to pre-1914.'

My first effort at letter-writing actually appeared in *The Christian Herald* on September 17, 1949. I was then just eight years old. It was nothing nearly as controversial as the 'City Gent' letter and just told of a two-week family holiday in Liverpool.

Despite my limited success as a scribe, my parents were dead-set against my becoming a journalist.

'Look, son,' said my father patiently, 'we hear that people who work on newspapers drink, smoke and swear. We wouldn't want you involved with people of that sort.'

'But . . .'.

'No buts!'

Nervous giggles from thirty girls, pencils already sharpened, greeted me as I walked scarlet-faced into the classroom. I suppose being the only boy on such a course for the next twelve months would be some red-blooded male's idea of heaven. To me it was, to start with at least, a time of excruciating embarrassment.

My mother had felt that I was really cut out for office life and so had encouraged me to enrol for a one-year secretarial course at Queensbridge School.

'But, Mum, shorthand and typing?' I protested. 'Everyone will think I'm a sissy.'

'No, they won't,' she said firmly. 'And if they do, they will have me to deal with.'

I was allowed to skip my fourth year at secondary school altogether and at the tender age of fourteen-and-a-half years I joined the horde of girls on the school's first-ever secretarial course. I figured that if I ever fulfilled my ambition of becoming a reporter, the shorthand and typing would be important.

But as the course continued, I began to believe that this was all futile. What kind of life lay ahead of me if I was just a clerk in an office? Surely, I could become a journalist and travel the world.

'No, son, we don't want you to become a journalist,' was my mother's abrupt reaction.

'Well, if I can't do that, I'm going to leave school now. I don't want to work in an office all my life.' It was now November, 1955, and I was, by law, allowed to leave school in a few weeks.

My mother was concerned about my rebellious spirit which was being exhibited in regular clashes at home. So she took me to see the school principal, Miss Marjorie Mason, a large, forceful woman who took a dim view of my plans for leaving.

'Wooding,' she said as she fixed her piercing eyes on mine, 'you will never succeed in anything in life if you give up at the first hurdle. If you want to become a journalist, you first have to learn shorthand and typing.'

'But, Miss Mason, my parents don't want me to be a journalist.'

'Oh,' she said, looking at my mother. 'Is that so?'

My mother's face became red with embarrassment. 'Well . . . err . . . we would prefer him to go into a nice office . . . .'

'Well,' said the principal turning her broad face to mine, 'the future lies in your hands. You either leave now a failure or you show your backbone and fight back. And who knows where that will lead? Your dreams may one day come true.'

With that I felt I had no alternative but to continue at the school. Her talk had been the jolt I had needed. I had spent too much time lately dreaming, I now had to do something to make those dreams happen.

I stood shaking with nerves outside the principal's office. A messenger had come to our classroom to ask me to appear before her immediately.

I rapped twice at the door of her office in the foyer of

the school and her deep voice boomed, 'Enter.'

She did not look up immediately, but had her nose buried in a pile of papers. After about a minute, in which I felt my heart was about to blow up, she looked up.

'Oh, Wooding,' she said in a voice that sent shivers up and down my spine. 'I have something to say to you.'

I gulped.

'Yes, I'm glad you decided to stay on and complete the course. You've certainly worked hard. You've won first prize for the most improved student in the fifth year. Congratulations! Go after that dream.'

I was in a daze. Maybe dreams could come true, even in Birmingham?

5

Canada Calling

Experience is the best of schoolmasters, only the school fees
are heavy.

THOMAS CARLYLE

The airmail letter flopped through our Birmingham letter-
box and I quickly scooped it up. I was usually waiting by
the front door for the mail to be delivered, because I had
been engaging in a rather torrid letter-writing campaign
with Sharon, my American pen-pal in Minnesota. I certainly didn't want my parents to read any of this ardent
material. But this one had a Toronto postmark on it, so I
knew it must be from Jenny, a friend I had met at a dance
that my parents had not found out about.

The correspondence had arrived just three months after
Jenny had headed off to Canada. She was ecstatic about
life in this new country.

'Dan,' she wrote, 'this place is great. Much better than
grotty old Birmingham. Why not come over? You'll have
a ball.'

Toronto. What a thought! I looked it up on the map. It
was just ninety miles from the US border, so I could hop
down there regularly and see what America was really

46

like. And, of course, I would be able at last to meet up with the amazing Sharon.

I switched on the record player in my bedroom and waited for Rick Nelson's 'Poor Little Fool' to drop onto the turntable. I lay there quietly contemplating my big move. That room itself, with its bare gas fire and bay window that overlooked our tiny back yard, had come to symbolize for me that I was very much alone. I had few real friends, and little or no communication with my sister Ruth, by now a born-again Christian, or my parents.

My thoughts were rudely interrupted when my father thumped on the door and yelled, 'Turn that racket down. It's driving us all crazy.'

The 'racket' drowned out my response: 'Well, you won't be having to put up with it much longer. I'm off to a better life.'

I smiled as I pondered the fact that I would no longer have to be afflicted with interminable services at the Mission—the cloistered centre of the universe for my family. There would be no more days at the boring city-centre office where I now worked as a clerk. An approach to the local newspapers had all resulted in the response I had expected, 'You do not have enough academic qualifications.'

Without telling my family, I took a day off work and caught a bus to London to visit the Canadian Embassy. There I collected brochures about life in Canada and discovered what formalities needed to be gone through to emigrate there.

Toronto certainly seemed an attractive proposition and I was in a consuming hurry to get there. It was an ungovernable urge.

'But you can't leave us like this.' My mother was distraught when she caught me reading my emigration literature and I confessed that I planned to leave as soon as the formalities were completed.

'I not only can, but I will!' I said callously. 'I've had enough of you all—and God. I'm going to see what the rest of the world is like. It can't be any worse than here.'

It was a sad little group consisting of my parents, Ruth and Aunt Ethel that, in March, 1960, gathered at Birmingham International Airport to see me off. My father blinked back the tears as he held me close and said, 'God be with you, son. We'll be praying for you.' I nodded, but said nothing. After all, wasn't it to escape the restrictions of my parents' religion that I was leaving home?

A lump gnawed at my stomach and my eyes were hot and moist as I went through to board the small plane that would carry me to London, where later that day I would catch the connection to Toronto. There was no turning back.

We touched down in Toronto some eighteen hours later, after a short refuelling stop. The stairs were put up against the aircraft and I literally ran down them. I was nearly knocked sideways by an icy blast of wind. The formalities were efficient and polite. A stamp in my passport confirmed that I was now a 'landed immigrant'.

The immigration official handed me back my passport. 'I hope it all works out well for you in our country,' he said, smiling mechanically. 'And have a nice day.'

I thanked him and then collected my bags and staggered through customs under the weight of the two cases. As I went through the barrier, I spotted the composed, mannequinlike figure of Jenny immediately. We both grinned broadly.

'Well, I've gone and done it now, Jenny,' I said as she planted a kiss on my cheek. She could see a look of both excitement and bewilderment on my face.

'Don't worry at all. You're going to love it here.'

I wanted so much to believe her, and stammered out my thanks for coming out to meet me. Already gone was her Birmingham accent, and it was replaced with a strange hybrid which sounded more North American than Brummie.

Over coffee, she began giving me advice on life in Toronto, 'By the way,' she said casually, 'how much money did you bring with you?'

I pulled out my wallet and counted out ten five-dollar notes.

'I make that precisely fifty dollars,' I said, holding them up.

Jenny stared, thunderstruck at my naîvety.

'You mean to say that's all you've brought to start a new life?'

'Well, it was all I could rake up.'

'Dan, are you completely crazy? You'll not last five minutes on that.'

I could see she was already beginning to regret giving me the postal hard-sell on life in Toronto. We hardly spoke on the bus journey, then she directed me to the immigration office where I had been instructed to report. As I stood in the gusting, icy, snow-leadened air with the wind clawing at my face, I felt the chill of loneliness envelop me.

Where was the glamour of Toronto that I had expected? All I could see then in 1960 was a few rather feeble skyscrapers, a lot of shabby shops, and cars covered in all the filth of the tail-end of winter. The city looked even more depressing than Birmingham.

The immigration officer had a bored expression as I sat down opposite him.

'I don't know why you've bothered to come, Mr Wooding,' he said, speaking in a monotone as he tipped back in his chair. 'There is a great shortage of jobs here at this time. You'll be lucky to get anything.'

With that he told me to return in a few days. He was obviously eager to terminate the conversation, and I felt as if I had been hit in the stomach.

I headed out into the biting wind and felt like screaming. Why were people so apparently hostile? What had I done that was so very wrong?

The hotel that I had to check into was like something from an old movie. The decrepit clerk took my government voucher which entitled me to stay free of charge for the first two nights. He picked up my suitcases and wheezed his way up to the first floor, where my room was located.

'Don't be surprised if you get a knock on your door during the middle of the night,' he grinned toothlessly. 'There are some very naughty ladies who like to visit this hotel. Have a nice night!'

I sat on the creaking bed in my small room that had a barracks flavour about it, and turned on the radio. Elvis' 'Heartbreak Hotel' came crackling out, and that certainly didn't help my state of mind. I took a deep breath and clenched and unclenched my right fist. I was fighting anger and confusion, and was losing.

What was I doing in Canada? What was I running away from? I was the 'Poor Little Fool' that Rick Nelson had been singing about.

I finally undressed. Eventually I drifted off, and slept fitfully.

When I woke next morning I jumped up with a start. I rubbed my eyes and realized I was not in my little room back home, but in a strange and foreign land.

Two days later, I needed to find new accommodation. I managed to get a room at the Central YMCA. This place was certainly much better than the hotel, but it did not provide individual radios in the rooms. So I rather foolishly joined the life ebbing and flowing up and down Yonge Street, Toronto's largest thoroughfare, and bought myself a transistor radio.

Then I phoned Jenny,

'Hi, Dan. How's everything?' She seemed friendly, although I still couldn't get used to her newly-acquired North American accent.

'Yes, everything's fine.' I paused momentarily, and then added, 'Well . . . except for the fact that I'm broke. I've spent my last dollars on a radio.'

'You've what?'

We arranged an urgent meeting and I shamefacedly told Jenny how my fifty dollars had 'just disappeared' on food, accommodation and the radio.

'You probably think I'm crazy, Jenny, but I couldn't face the loneliness of my room without a radio.'

Instead of blowing up, she took my hand and said gently, 'Look, Dan, I encouraged you to come over, so I'll help you all I can. I'll organize a collection at the hostel where I'm staying, and we'll give you a loan. But don't go wasting any more of it.'

She had brought with her a copy of one of Toronto's newspapers, and began searching the accommodation columns.

'We have got to find you an inexpensive place that will give you full board.'

I went back to the YMCA canteen and sat and drank my umpteenth cup of tea. I was so low that I even seriously considered packing my bags there and then and leaving for home—whatever the consequences. I had run away from my parents and the constant conflicts; also the Mission, but most of all from God. Life, it had seemed to me, as a Christian was incredibly boring and irrelevant. But was this any better? I felt like hurling my cup across the room in utter frustration. Then Jenny's voice cut in as she returned from the pay-phone.

'Okay, Dan, get packed. I've got you a place to stay,' she said, smiling broadly. 'It's in the High Park area, which is one of the better parts of Toronto. You'll get a private room and loads of food.'

The tram dropped us off at the end of High Park Boulevard, and we began walking down this delightful tree-lined road, full of large detached houses and well-manicured lawns.

'That's yours,' said Jenny, pointing to a large solid house. It was red-bricked and had white pillars at the front of it supporting the structure.

Greta, the gracefully slim Austrian 'hostess' greeted us at the doorway and showed me my tiny room, which at least was clean and tidy.

The other guests were definitely not friendly. They turned out to be mainly German and made it obvious to me that an Englishman was not 'velcome' in their Teutonic world. No one sat with me at the breakfast table, and they all jabbered away in German in little groups.

Once again a desperate loneliness overwhelmed me. I had, by now, become so low that I would lie on my bed for hours wishing my life would come to an abrupt end. It was an unhappiness I could not handle at all.

Then, five weeks to the day that I had arrived, I finally got a job. The immigration office put me in touch with an insurance company where I was offered the position of accounts clerk at fifty dollars a week.

After two faltering months at the insurance job, I was slowly getting my confidence back, and was even cracking jokes with some of the staff, many of whom were also recent immigrants.

However, I was not prepared for what happened on the Monday of the ninth week when I came downstairs for my breakfast with the Germans. I noticed they were all standing around in agitated groups mouthing Germanic oaths.

'What's happened?' I enquired.

'The lady who ran this place has run off with all the downstairs furniture,' said one of the exasperated Germans. 'Her boyfriend must have come late last night with his van and helped her load it. She's done a midnight flit.'

Another added: 'I know she was owed back wages by the guy who owned the place, so I suppose she decided to take the law into her own hands and take what she felt she was owed.'

So that was it. We were all homeless.
I ran to the nearby pay-phone and got Jenny on the line.
'Yes, Dan, what is it this time?'
'You'll never believe this . . . .'
'Go on . . . try me!'

6

Trouble in Toronto

There is a certain relief in change, even though it be from bad to worse; as I have found in traveling in a stage coach, that it is often a comfort to shift one's position and be bruised in a new place.

WASHINGTON IRVING

It could have been providence, I don't know. But Alan, the brother of Beth, one of the girls whom I used to see at the lunchtime rock-and-roll dance sessions I secretly attended at the Casino, Birmingham, had arrived in Toronto. He had contacted me and told me that he had moved into what he called a 'super apartment'.

'Why don't you come and share it?' he suggested on hearing of my predicament.

'There's three of us already, and I'm sure the others wouldn't mind a fourth at all. After all, us Brummies have got to stick together.'

We each had our own bedroom, and I got on well with Alan and the others, both Canadians. So with a new base I could begin to enjoy life in Toronto. I found a soccer team to play with—Piccadilly United—and was settling into my job. So it was quite a shock to me when I got home from the office, just six weeks after moving in, and the voluble landlady met me on the doorstep.

'Mr Wooding.' She was obviously in a serious mood. 'I am sorry to tell you that there has been a complaint against you by the others,' she said in a sharp, accusing tone.

'Complaint?'

'Yes, I'm afraid they feel you haven't been doing your share of the washing up.'

I broke into a chuckle.

'But that's not true. Well, I may have missed on a few occasions.'

'I don't want to argue with you,' she cut in. 'I just want you to pack up your things and leave. I'm giving you one week's notice to find somewhere else to live.'

She wasn't joking as I had first thought, and I was numb with shock. The others were quite embarrassed with the situation, but obviously they had got together and decided that for some reason they wanted me out. They already had somebody else to take my place.

As I went to my room, I found a letter waiting for me from my mother. Since I had arrived in Canada, she had bombarded me with endless airmail epistles. Mostly they were snippets about life at the Mission.

'Everyone is praying for you there,' she wrote this time.

I usually skipped quickly past these parts of the letters, but I couldn't ignore her comments about my father's health, all apparently resulting from his problems in Nigeria.

'He's been really poorly,' she said. 'I don't know how much longer he will be able to continue at the Mission. I think things are more serious than he lets on.'

Fortunately, that night I had a soccer game for Piccadilly United. I hoped that would help lift the gloom. During half-time I mentioned to the rest of the team that I was in desperate need of accommodation.

Jack Loughran, our Ulster-born right winger, came

over to me.

'Dan, I've got room in my basement flat. Why don't you move in with me. We can share the rent. What do you say then?'

'What can I say, but thanks! Can I move in tonight?'

Life with Jack, a kindly bachelor in his early thirties, was a pleasure. He was a Roman Catholic who was extremely tolerant of other views. He loved sports and pop music, as I did, so we got on like a house on fire.

With the constant pressure from my mother to start going to church again, I thought I had better make a few token visits to keep her happy. One Sunday, I listened to a live service from the People's Church in Bloor Street on the radio, and I decided to go there the following week.

I caught the tube and made my way into the old building that then housed the church. I felt a strange glow that morning as I heard old, familiar hymns again. I had actually brought along the Bible that my mother had given me at Birmingham Airport and followed the Scripture reading.

The preacher looked like an Old Testament prophet with his long white flowing locks. He was Dr Oswald J. Smith, a world-famous preacher whom Billy Graham once described as 'the greatest combination pastor, hymn writer, missionary statesman, and evangelist of our time'. I cannot remember what Dr Smith spoke about that morning, but I can remember being astonished that he issued a morning 'altar call'. Many people went forward to the front to accept Christ.

As I watched, I could almost feel my white-haired mother squeezing my arm and whispering as she had done on many occasions before, 'Go forward, son. Now's your chance to get right with the Lord.' But I wouldn't. My pride wouldn't allow it.

Sunday after Sunday I joined the large congregation at the church. During one service, two robed members of the choir actually came from their stalls to decide for Christ.

That took real courage—something I didn't have. They had publicly admitted they had been living a lie.

Jack used to get on to me and ask, 'Dan, why do you keep going to that church?'

I told him I didn't really know, but that there was something special going on there and I was hoping some of it would one day rub off on me.

After eleven months in my job my departmental boss, Chuck, called me over to his desk.

'Well,' he paused as if not quite knowing how to phrase what he had to say. 'You see . . . well look, there's been a complaint against you,' he continued, tapping his foot nervously.

'Complaint?' I was mystified. 'Haven't I been doing my share of the washing up then?'

He looked puzzled. 'No,' he said acrimoniously, 'it's just that some of the girls here say that you have BO.'

'BO?' I was shocked and hurt at being labelled a villain.

'Yes, they feel you should clean up your act and start using a more powerful deodorant.'

He paused to allow his words to sink in.

For a moment I sat there blinking, not totally comprehending what he had said. Then an angry flush began to climb up the back of my neck. Why, I thought, should I take this from these silly people.

'But this place is like a sauna. You have the heating far too high . . . and . . . .'

Chuck raised his hands to try and forestall my torrent of rage.

My voice rose three octaves as I shouted, 'Okay, Chuck, I'll just go and have three showers, one after the other. Is that okay with you?' In the heat of anger I stood up and addressed the office. 'Okay with all of you?' I yelled.

That night, Jack and I began discussing our respective lives in Canada over a few drinks.

'I can't see what I'm doing here, Jack. They say at work that I stink. Well, I think this whole place stinks. They treat you like you're a criminal rather than someone who has come to help build up their country.'

'Now, hold on, Dan. Canada's been good to me.'

He could see I was just about all in. 'Don't you think you've had enough to drink tonight, Dan? Sleep on it. You'll probably feel better in the morning.'

I lay in the darkness, breathing heavily, waiting for honest sleep to blot it all away. It didn't. For next morning, another letter came from my mother. I groaned as I ripped it open, knowing that it would contain at least three sermonettes.

But this time, it didn't!

'Dan, your father collapsed while preaching at the Mission last Sunday and the doctor says he thinks he's got cancer.

'If you feel you can, please come home quickly. It may be the last chance to see your dad alive.'

There was a pathetic urgency in her tone. What should I do? I felt conflicting emotions: sadness for my father, and anger with Canada—an anger born of frustration and humiliation. But if I returned home, I knew I would have to admit that I had made a mess of my decision to move to Canada. But still, there seemed little alternative.

With shaking hands I picked up the phone and dictated a cable to my mother. 'I'll be home as soon as possible. Love, Dan.'

The icebergs from our windy vantage point at the rail of the *Empress of Canada* looked both menacing and magnificent. A flock of seagulls stood motionless on one of them.

Jack looked vacant. 'Dan,' he mused, 'what have you got me into? Life was safe in Toronto. Now you've got me moving to England to start all over again.'

Our regular conversations back at the apartment had

resulted in our making a joint decision to leave Canada and head back to England. I would naturally go to Birmingham, and he would try his luck in London.

'I suppose,' he conceded, 'I had got into something of a rut. But life was safe.'

I knew that I, too, was taking a risk heading back home. I would have to swallow my pride and start attending services at the Mission again. I guessed that people I had known would label my emigration attempt as a disaster and, to a great extent, it was.

But really I was going home out of a sense of guilt. I could not have remained in Canada while my father was so ill. He was going through a real nightmare. Because of his past record of tropical illness, he had been making regular visits to see a consultant at a Birmingham hospital. The doctor had conducted a series of tests over a period of months. He wanted to discover why my father was always in such pain and why he suffered constantly from diarrhoea. It was during one such visit that the specialist had finally told him, 'I'm afraid you have cancer.'

The shock was like a knife that drove deep into his mind. He sat there stunned, trying to take in what the specialist had said.

'We'll have to operate on you,' added the doctor. 'Otherwise, you've got a maximum of three months to live.'

My father stumbled from the hospital towards the bus to take him home. How could he break such terrible news to his wife and Ruth? He climbed on board, paid the fare and withdrew into himself. He sat there, unaware of his surroundings, praying silently: 'Lord, not cancer. Please, not cancer.'

Mother knew something serious was up when he walked through the door. She brewed up a cup of tea and said, 'Come on, Alf, what's wrong?'

The whole story came tumbling out. She was stunned, yet she knew the strain of his years of illness could not go on for ever and was relieved that something was to be done.

'Never mind, Alf. There is a scripture that talks about everything working together for good to those who love God. I believe that, and you must too.'

Her eyes held his. 'Anyway,' she said gently. 'I believe this news will mean that Dan will be home soon and we'll see a big change in him.'

'Maybe . . .' he smiled weakly. 'Maybe . . . .'

7

The Prodigal Returns

Salvation is moving from living death to deathless life.

JACK ODELL

The Liver Building rose up majestically in the silent, muffled world of white, salty, drifting fog of that Liverpool morning. There was a damp sting in the air as I stood peering through the mist at the crowds of people excitedly waiting dockside, and as the crew began to tie up the *Empress,* the white-haired figure of my mother, came into view. She was with the more substantial form of her sister, Ethel, and they were both waving madly at me. I felt tears well up in my eyes as I waved back.

I was home!

A motherly hug greeted me as I tumbled through the exit of the rather shabby customs shed.

'How is Dad? Is he still alive?' There was a big lump in my throat.

My mother looked frailer than I had ever seen her. Her face was milk white. But her still grey-blue eyes locked onto mine. They were as steady as ever.

'He's very ill. But your coming back will really buck him up.' I introduced Jack to her and then he headed out for his new life in England.

My favourite aunt, Ethel, then greeted me with a kiss. Later, when my mother was out of earshot, she said, 'Dan, you've done the right thing. Your parents have been pining for you. You don't know how much they have missed you.'

'But,' I said mystified, 'I caused them so much trouble.'

'Yes,' she explained patiently, 'but you are still their son and they love you.'

My father looked gaunt, but managed to smile as I came into the lounge. He was wearing a dressing gown and shakily got to his feet as I walked in. He seemed unsure as to whether he should hug me or just shake hands. He settled for a gentle handshake.

'Welcome home, son,' he said, his lips pale and quivering with emotion. 'I've really missed you. You'll find your rock-and-roll records are a bit worn out, but otherwise your room is still the same.'

I looked at him, a quizzical look on my face.

'Do you mean to say you've been playing my records? But you hated them!'

He allowed a thin smile to pass over his face. 'When you left, I missed you so much that I would go up to your room and play the records and imagine you were still here. I liked Pat Boone the best.'

I couldn't hold back any longer. 'Oh, Dad, I can't tell you how much I've missed you and Mum.'

A week before Christmas, 1961, my father was admitted to the Queen Elizabeth Hospital in Birmingham. It was life or death for him. The cancer would have to be cut away.

We visited him daily and, each time, before we left home, my mother and Ruth implored God to help him. I sat quietly looking on, but not participating. One day, just before the operation, I broke down. 'Mum,' I sobbed, 'I'm not worthy to ask God to heal Dad.' I had reached the point of desperation.'

At his bedside on the morning of the surgery, I felt like weeping again. The lines of strain around his mouth showed up more than ever. His cheeks had become hollow with the skin taut over his facial bones. He was thin enough for me to see the recoil of his heart after each beat. He looked so tired, so close to eternity. But as I gazed at his face, integrity was etched into every line. His faith was still strong. That was important to me.

'Dan,' he said in a tremulous voice as his weak, white-knuckled hand gripped mine, 'thank you for coming home.' His voice was very low now, hardly audible. 'I may not come out of this alive, but whatever happens, I hope we will meet again—in heaven.' He tried to say more but his voice would not co-operate. I stood there for a few long moments. There were no words but the communication was total.

With that, he was wheeled into the operating theatre, not knowing if he would come out alive and I experienced the stabbing pain of guilt. With a feeling of helplessness, I watched my father's slight figure disappear down the corridor in an almost funereal way.

The ward nurse told us sympathetically that it would be a long operation, and we should go home and wait.

'Maybe,' she said gently, 'you could phone in about six hours. It should be over by then.'

When we arrived home on that icy winter's day, I headed straight up the stairs to my bedroom. The barn-like room was freezing and I inserted sixpence into the gas meter and then lit the fire. I felt unable to talk to Ruth and my mother. I needed solitude.

As I paced the room, tears began to tumble down my flushed cheeks. I had run away like the prodigal son in the Bible. I had caused much pain to my parents, and now my father was facing death and I knew I might never see him again.

'Lord, I don't want to say good-bye for ever to my dad,' I beseeched God as I prowled around like a caged tiger.

Suddenly the very air was crammed and vibrating with electric potential and my weak ankles almost buckled. Without thinking, I sank to my knees at my bedside and cried out my apologies to God for all the wrongs I had done in my twenty years of life that had taken me to three continents. My breath wrenched out of my lungs in painful sobs. In the stillness my heart was beating audibly in my ears.

'Lord, I believe, I really believe in you.' I wiped away the tears with my grey woolly sweater before I could continue.

'I don't know if I will see my father again in this life but, please, I want to see him again in glory.

'Forgive me for my rotten, selfish past. My temper, my anger, my pride and rebellion. Please wash away my sins and, please . . . please, take over my life.

'Use me and, if it is your will, please spare the life of my dad.'

I must have been on my knees for half and hour. Finally, I rose to my feet and walked unsteadily into the bathroom and threw cold water on my face to wash away the tears. Then I slowly closed the door behind me and went downstairs where my mother and Ruth were deep in conversation. All at once I wanted to laugh and cry and to shout aloud.

'What's up, Dan?' called my sister timidly, seeing my blotchy features. 'You look as if you've been crying. That's not like you.'

'Well, I've gone and done it. I asked Jesus to forgive me and come into my life.'

They both looked stunned.

'Cheer up, Mum,' I added, a smile appearing on my tear-stained face, my eyes gleaming. 'It could have been worse. I could have gone forward at one of those awful Youth for Christ rallies you used to drag me along to at the Town Hall.' With that I pulled a mock, stern face.

Her tense face visibly relaxed as she got the joke! We all

broke into unrestrained laughter and then threw our arms around each other. We were not an emotional family, but we all felt this was a time to let it all out! The pent-up flood of emotion released itself at last. As I laughed out loud I realized how little joy there had been in my life over the past year.

Time seemed to fly as, at last, we had this bond of being a united Christian family. Ruth had made her commitment to Christ some years previously. Words of joy rushed out from all of us.

I suddenly glanced at my watch and said, 'Come on, Mum, let's go to the phone box down the street and call the hospital. Surely, they'll have some news for us.'

The three of us put on our coats and headed out into that Birmingham winter's night to the call box.

Ruth and I were standing in the icy wind, swinging our arms against the cold as my mother made the call and the nurse came on the line. I could see the slight colour rise in my mother's cheeks as the conversation continued.

'He's survived the operation and is back in the ward,' she said with tears brimming. 'The nurse says he's very weak but, praise God, he's alive.'

'Thank you, Jesus,' I yelled. Somehow this type of language which had once made me shudder now seemed right. I felt intensely alive.

'Thank you, Lord!'

As we walked home, I said to Mum, 'I saw your cheeks redden as you said something on the phone to the nurse. What was it?'

'Tell him,' my mother answered, 'our Prodigal has finally come home. He'll understand.'

I felt a choking sensation in the base of my throat, and again the sharp sting of tears.

'You know,' she said, turning to me, her face bright with excitement, 'this is the best Christmas present we could ever have had. God has saved both of you.'

8

Our Norma

We are shaped and fashioned by what we love.

GOETHE

It was hard for me to take my eyes off the raven-haired beauty who sat engrossed in her accounting books at the other side of the glass partition that divided our offices. She had short black hair, a thin elegant nose, and large brown eyes. Her delicate olive-skin face had a hint of Latin about it.

We had met in the far-from-romantic surroundings of a company that manufactured cycle dynamos. It was housed in a crumbling building in the Aston district of Birmingham. Jobs, in the early sixties, were hard to come by in this city. I had been to a labour exchange to discover what jobs there were, but I didn't exactly get off to a good start. I had held out my hand to the officer there and he had studied it as if it were some dubious foreign object.

'What would you really like to do?' he finally asked, trying to sound chatty.

'I'd like to be a journalist,' I said brightly, hoping he would immediately phone the *Birmingham Evening Mail* and arrange an interview for me.

He offered a dry smile and peered through his rimless glasses at my qualifications which showed I could type and I had learned shorthand, and that was just about it.

'Well, son,' he said tonelessly, trying to stifle a yawn and shuffling the papers in front of him, 'I would think the best I could do for you with these qualifications is get you a job as a clerk in a factory. It pays ten pounds a week. How does that sound to you?'

I looked at him sharply. He looked back levelly. The 'job' he had in mind meant that I would be earning less than when I left for Canada some twelve months earlier. It was as if God was telling me that I must now start out on a pilgrimage and, although some of it would not be pleasant, I had to be obedient, patient, and learn to walk with him. Wherever he led me, I must go.

I got the position and the bus journey from Kings Heath, with a change in the city-centre, took an hour. I would use the time to read my Bible. Being brought up in a Christian family meant I knew the Scriptures quite well, but they had never come alive for me before.

During a particularly tiresome journey I fluttered the pages of my black leather-bound Bible and my eyes rested on the story, in Genesis, about the creation of Eve.

I read in Genesis 2:20—'The man gave names to all cattle, and to the birds of the air, and to every beast of the field; but for man there was not found a helper fit for him.'

I read on: 'Therefore a man leaves his father and his mother and cleaves to his wife, and they become one flesh' (verse 24).

As I closed my Bible, completely oblivious of the people sitting around me talking or reading a morning paper, I began to pray silently.

'Lord, you know how lonely I've been over the past years; it's been terrible. Now I realize that I need a 'helper' to be with me so that we can serve you together.'

My mother had constantly been trying to interest me in

girls who came to the Mission, but none of them had really taken my attention.

Now Norma, the raven-haired slightly-built girl who sat behind the glass, was different.

'Is she the one for me, Lord?' I asked on the bus. 'If so, please give me the courage to ask her out.'

For nearly two months I tried to speak to her. But somehow the words would just dry up in my throat.

'Lord,' I said quietly in the office one day, as the type-writers clattered, 'I need courage now. Show me what to do.'

I went to the antiquated adding-machine in another office to total the day's orders, and found Norma sitting at another accounting machine inputting data. I tried to make desultory conversation, but again I froze. My knuckles went white with tension. But eventually I was able to speak.

'Norma.' She turned and looked at me. Her skin was radiant, her eyes bright.

'You have the sort of face only a mother could love.'

My nerves had caused me to repeat something that a friend had once said to me at school. I don't know why. Unless, of course, the Lord had a sense of humour.

There was a moment of shocked silence and then she responded, 'I beg your pardon.'

I put my hand over my mouth to cover my embarrassment.

Then I did it again. 'Norma, that's what I like about you—NOTHING!'

Her eyes met mine, and both of us got the giggles. The tension had gone and I was still chuckling as I returned to my desk.

I reached into my briefcase and pulled out some writing paper and began forming a letter to her. She has kept it to this day. It read:

Dear Norma,

Hi! As I am a bit of a coward in asking nice girls for dates, I wondered if I could ask you, through this letter, if you would do me the honour of coming out with me tomorrow night or, if you can't make it, then one night next week.

I have been wanting to ask you out for a long time but didn't quite know how to do it, so at last I have decided to ask you and I do hope you will say *yes!*

If you do say *yes,* can you let me know where you would like to go (any place you like) and it shall be arranged.

I slipped into her office and, while she was talking to another girl, left it on her desk. The envelope said, 'To Our Norma.'

I felt a flush spread across my cheeks as she looked at me shyly through the partition. 'Yes,' she mouthed, her eyes glistening. 'I'll go out with you. I thought you'd never ask.'

We went to see a film the next night. It was about homosexuals, and we had to sit apart because the cinema was packed to capacity. We both laughed about such a bizarre start to our relationship. Outside her terraced home in Aston we kissed without touching, and I ran to get my bus back home.

'Lord,' I said as the late-night drunks staggered on and off the bus at each stop, 'I want to thank you for my future wife. I am now going to open my Bible again, and I would ask you to speak to me through it.'

I just rustled the pages of the pocket-sized Bible and came to John 15:7, 'If you abide in me, and my words abide in you, ask whatever you will, and it shall be done for you.'

'Lord,' I whispered, 'I asked for a helpmate, and you gave me one tonight. I accept that verse as your confirmation.'

I spent most of my spare time with Norma, and even went back to her home at lunchtime to eat my corned-beef sandwiches and to talk with her parents, Howard and Maud. However, I found it almost impossible to share with her my faith.

One day, we were walking along hand-in-hand when we passed a Gospel Hall with the sign prominently displayed, 'God so loved the world that he gave his only begotten son.'

'I used to go there to Sunday School,' Norma remarked as her voice wavered a little. 'I loved it.'

Then she looked quizzically at me. 'Aren't you religious, Dan? I've seen you reading your Bible at your desk during the break.' Her eyes held mine steadily.

'Yes, well not exactly religious. I'm a Christian. There is a difference!'

She squeezed my hand affectionately and said, 'Tell me about it. How did you become a Christian?' There was a rapt attention on her face as she turned her eyes on mine.

Out poured the whole story of my rebellion, my trip to Canada, my intense loneliness, and my father's illness, from which he had made a remarkable recovery.

'My dad's doing fine, really fine,' I assured her. 'He's now back doing a little preaching at the Mission, where he's the pastor.'

'But why won't you introduce me to your parents?'

'I will—one day. But I didn't want to put you off.'

I had to admit that although I had asked the Lord to find me this wife I still feared she would ditch me if she thought either me or my family were 'religious nuts'.

After taking Norma out for two months, I bought myself a Lambretta scooter. We would go out together on it, and I would ride on Sunday night from the evening service to her home.

I also used it for work each day. But, as I was to discover to my cost, scooters in frosty weather can be lethal. One night, returning home from Aston, I found myself driving through tendrils of freezing mist, as white and fine as floating lace. Too late I saw a red traffic light and

slammed on the brakes. As if in slow motion, the whole
machine slid away at the back and I crashed headlong
onto the road. Fortunately, there was no other traffic
around and I was wearing a helmet, so my head was protected. But as I hit the ground I felt a dart of pain in my
left leg. It was lacerated and bleeding. I managed to get
back on the machine, start it, and gingerly drive it home.

After my wound was cleansed by my mother, I asked
Dad to do me a favour.

'I expect you've guessed that I have a girlfriend at work.
She's lovely. Her name is Norma. I wonder if you would
phone her tomorrow and tell her what's happened. Explain that I'll be away for a few days.'

'Of course I will,' he said gently. 'Why don't you invite
her over?'

The next night Norma sat at my bedside clasping my
shaking hand. My parents fussed around her, and my
sister and Norma hit it off straightaway. When we were
alone, Norma turned to me and said, 'Your family aren't
the slightest bit strange as you led me to believe. I'd like to
start going to the Mission with you.'

"Done!' We shook hands on the deal.

Our wedding took place on July 13, 1963, at Aston Parish
Church. We could have been married in the Mission, but
with so many friends and members of the family wanting
to attend, we felt the little hall would not accommodate so
many people.

It was a beautiful occasion, without any hitches. But as
we sped away on the train to Babbacombe, Devon, I had
an uneasy feeling that something was not quite right with
our relationship. What could it be? We loved each other
and could hardly bear to be apart.

The green fields outside the window were just a blur as
the train raced west. Norma took out a novel to read.
Strangely enough it was *From Here to Eternity*.

'Lord,' I whispered, 'please show me what is wrong. I

don't understand why I feel so uneasy.'

As Norma's eyes were glued to the novel, I got out my Bible and opened it at 2 Corinthians and my eyes stopped at verse fourteen of chapter six. There I read, 'Do not be mismated with unbelievers. For what partnership have righteousness and iniquity? Or what fellowship has light with darkness?'

I closed my Bible and allowed those words to sink into my mind. I was confused. Although I was convinced that God had brought us together; I knew Norma was not a believer in the biblical sense. I felt the Lord was saying to me, 'Yes, I did bring you together, but you will never be able to serve me properly until she, too, has committed her life to me.'

I leaned over to Norma and asked, 'Darling, are you a Christian?'

She looked up puzzled from her book and threw a quick, startled glance at my face.

'That's a funny question to ask on our honeymoon,' she said after a long moment of awkward silence. 'Of course I am. I love going to the Mission and I say my prayers at night.'

'Yes, I know all of that, but the Bible talks about being "born again". Have you had that experience?'

'Well . . . no . . . ..' Her voice trailed off.

We had this conversation several times during the rain-splashed week of our honeymoon in Babbacombe. Even as we gingerly lay cradled in each other's arms on the squeaky bed in our hotel room, we talked incessantly about what a living faith really was.

'I don't know if I'm ready yet,' she admitted one day as we huddled under an umbrella gazing out over the beautiful rain-lashed cliffs. 'Just don't put the pressure on me. If you really do believe in prayer, pray for me that I might find what you keep talking about.'

One day after we arrived back in Birmingham, Norma suggested we ought to go and visit her parents and give them the gifts we had bought for them in Babbacombe.

'Then we'll go and see Hilda and Joe,' she said. Norma had already told me of her great affection for this couple that lived close by.

'Hilda,' she told me, 'became my second mother. I used to confide in her all the time and each Sunday I would have dinner with her and her Welsh-born husband, Joe. It became a tradition.'

Hilda was a professional dressmaker and had lovingly spent many hours making Norma's beautiful wedding dress. As we pulled up on my scooter outside Norma's family home, she removed her helmet and said, 'Do you know that Hilda told me at the wedding that that day marked the end of an era. She said, "Norma, you'll never have Sunday dinner with us again."'

I knocked at the front door of their house and Norma's mother Maud answered it. She looked gaunt. Her eyes were dark from much tears. Well-defined lines of strain were about her mouth.

'What on earth is wrong, Mum?' asked Norma.

'Come and sit down. I've something to tell you.'

I joined Norma on the settee and squeezed her hand.

'What's up?' Norma was impatient.

'Hilda's dead.'

'What!'

'She died in a car crash in Wales the day after your wedding. Joe's still in hospital. He's seriously ill.'

Norma was numb with shock, unable at first to respond. She covered her eyes with her hands and began to weep deep, heartfelt sobs that shook her whole body.

'Oh, my God, not Hilda . . . .' Her face was bleak. Very bleak. I tried to console her, but it didn't help. It was a terrible moment. She looked at me with stricken eyes, and in the hysteria of the moment ran her hands through her hair.

That night, in bed in our new home on the upper two floors of my parents' home, she clutched me tight in the darkness with a fierce, panicky tightness.

'Dan,' she said, her eyes dark-circled and tear-streaked. 'Why has God allowed such a thing to happen? Why? Why?' There was desperation in her voice as her body moaned in protest at the extreme emotions she had recently experienced.

I kissed her tears. 'Maybe the Lord is slowly knocking away the props in your life so you can really trust only in him.'

9

Through the Gates of Splendour

Yesterday ended last night.

CYPRUS H.K. CURTIS

That Sunday night service at the Mission really shouldn't have been any different. It was quite routine for the guest speakers to be invited to take the preaching load off my father's still-fragile shoulders.

Usually it was not difficult to find a seat, but this night was different. Of course there were the usual 'missioners', but the place was also full of young people I had not seen before. Most wore sashes which were inscribed with the words, 'Ribbons of Faith.' They were from the Sparkbrook Elim Pentecostal Church and had been invited by my father to take the service.

Norma smiled eagerly. I knew she felt they would certainly make a colourful alternative to the succession of dour middle-aged preachers who had been occupying the pulpit recently.

After eighteen months of marriage, we had settled down to a relatively comfortable life. By this time I had left the cycle generator company and was earning the princely sum of fifteen pounds a week with an electrical

75

company in the Hockley district of the city. Andrew, our first son, had been born, and everyone agreed he was the 'spitting image of his father'.

Norma was well accepted by the regulars at the Mission. In fact, no one even questioned that she wasn't a Christian. She knew the strange lingo that evangelicals speak— 'the language of Zion'—and could mouth all the acceptable phrases.

But there was still an uneasiness between us. I didn't want to force her to make that final commitment, remembering all too well my own negative response to my mother's pressures at the Youth for Christ rallies held in the Birmingham Town Hall.

In the pulpit was Adrian Hawkes, a cherub-faced young man who led the 'Ribbons of Faith' outreach team. He cleared his throat and explained to our mainly aging congregation, that their group had been formed so they could 'reach out with the gospel to the people of Birmingham'.

He said in his slight Birmingham accent, 'Jesus' great commission in Mark 16:15 was, "Go into all the world and preach the gospel to the whole creation." That command isn't an optional extra, it's something we all, as Christians, have to do.

'I challenge you here tonight to join with us in evangelizing this city for Christ.' As he spoke I felt my face stiffen a little.

My sister Ruth, who was home for the weekend from her Teacher Training College in Lancashire, came over to me after the service.

'Dan, that was a great challenge,' she said full of enthusiasm. 'Let's go and talk to Adrian and see how we can help.'

The young preacher suggested we should go along that night to their 'Late Night Special', which took place each Sunday evening in the back hall of their church.

'Anything can happen at these meetings,' he warned. 'Most of our clientele are bikers in black leather. So be prepared for a shock. What we are doing is not easy and there can be violence.'

There was! But still the group shared the gospel to the noisy, heckling bikers who jeered, cheered and whistled, especially as the girls sang. And as the sermon was preached, Neanderthal grunts came from all over the room which was fast turning into bedlam.

'It's pretty wild here,' I breathlessly whispered to Ruth, who had been deep in prayer for the team.

'Yes,' she nodded, 'this is a whole different world from the comfortable rallies we are used to.'

As we left, Ruth and I discussed what we had seen, and what we had been challenged to do. We agreed this was real frontline evangelism. Then an idea began to form in my mind.

'Why don't we start our own work at the Mission?' I suggested as my voice wavered a little.

'But we hardly have any young people,' said Ruth. 'There's you, me and Norma . . . and that's about it.'

I nodded.

'Well, if the Lord is in this, he'll supply us with the "troops" we need,' I said. 'Otherwise this will never get off the ground.'

A few days later we met at my home with Adrian and a few of his leading evangelical 'storm troopers'. I told them that we wanted to form a team called the Messengers, and felt we should start with a coffee bar in the back hall of the Mission on Saturday nights. Adrian agreed to back us and I also made contact with Jim Harding, Director of Evangelism at the Birmingham Bible Institute (BBI), and he promised to commit some of his students for the first few Saturdays.

So, on a freezing January night in 1965, a group of about thirty of us began transforming the back hall into a coffee bar. There was a time of prayer and then teams went out in twos to the uninviting frost-laden streets of Sparkbrook to invite people to the meeting.

I stayed behind at the Mission to welcome them. We had prepared lots of steaming coffee, and a gospel group from another church was to supply the music. We had also rented a slide presentation on five American missionaries slain in January, 1956 by Auca Indians in Ecuador. Adrian Hawkes was to preach.

I hadn't expected any of the older members of the church to attend that first night, so I was surprised to see the frail figure of Elsie Budd shuffling in and leaning heavily on her stick as she eased her way towards us.

'I'm sorry I'm late,' she apologized breathlessly, 'but the icy pavements meant it has taken me longer to get here than usual.'

I looked at this behatted old lady, someone who in my teenage years had often provided me with Sunday lunch, and could have wept.

'But you shouldn't be out on a night like this,' I protested.

She looked gently at me.

'Dan, do you remember in Ezekiel 22, where the Lord had decided to destroy the land? It says in verse thirty, "And I sought for a man that should . . . stand in the gap before me for the land, that I should not destroy it: but I found none."'

I nodded.

'Well, you see, I've come to "stand in the gap" for you. I may be too old to talk to these young people who will be coming in, but I can pray while you and your friends are sharing Jesus.'

Soon people started coming in and the meeting began. There were none of the troubles of the 'Late Night Special', and Norma began serving coffee to everyone in the room.

She came and stood by me as the slide presentation on the murdered missionaries began. We clasped hands tightly as at the end a picture of the five martyrs was flashed on the screen. It showed them gathering around a tape recorder before they were killed and singing 'We Rest in Thee'.

They were speared to death by Aucas shortly after making this actual recording. There was a hushed silence as the lights came on. I could see that Norma had been particularly moved by their story.

Then Paula, a student from the BBI came over to ask Norma to accompany her to a nearby coffee bar. Paula and her husband Keith headed for the door and I squeezed Norma's hand reassuringly.

As I stood on the steps of the hall and watched them leave, I prayed that something great would happen to Norma that night.

At the Ladypool Road coffee bar, Norma listened with rapt attention as Paula shared her faith simply and sincerely. On their way back to the Mission, Paula turned to Norma and asked her earnestly, 'Have you ever given your life over to Christ?'

She hesitated for a moment. 'Well, not exactly, but I do pray and go to all the services with Dan. I think I'm a Christian.'

'It's no good to just think you are a Christian. You have to know! You have to have an assurance that you have made your peace with God.

'Let's go back to the Mission right now and you accept Christ into your life there.'

'Okay . . . I'll do it,' she said, after a long moment of awkward silence.

They slipped back into the sanctuary and there Norma asked God to forgive her sins and then invited Christ into her life.

I could see that something had happened by Norma's shining eyes as she came into the coffee bar where we were just clearing up.

Paula whispered in my ear, 'Dan, your wife has something to tell you.'

'Yes, love,' I said as I began putting chairs back in place

for the Sunday school next morning.

'I've done it . . . I've been born again by Jesus. I'm a Christian,' she said in a husky voice. Her lower lip quivered with emotion and there was a flush on her high cheekbones.

I took her in my arms. 'Norma, this is the happiest moment of my life. Now we can work together in whatever God has in mind for us.' Little did I know what he had in mind for us at that time!

10

Junkies Are People Too

There is nothing as easy as denouncing. It don't take much to
see something is wrong, but it does take some eyesight to see
what will put it right again.

WILL ROGERS

Bacon and eggs sizzled merrily in the pan as I switched on
the television. Norma was telling me about her day, when
I suddenly found my attention being drawn to the screen
where a doctor from a local drug clinic was being inter-
viewed.

'We need people to come and visit our recovering
addicts,' said the doctor. 'They are being weaned off drugs
and get very jumpy, so visitors would really help them and
us.'

'Did you hear that?' I found my heart beginning to race.
'He's asking for visitors.'

Norma smiled sanguinely. She had got used to my enthusiasm for just about everything I got involved in.

'You're not thinking of volunteering the Messengers to
go into that clinic?'

I nodded with a smile.

'But you know nothing about drug addiction,' she

81

countered in her practical way.

I laughed. 'When has that ever stopped me doing any-thing?' I chuckled. 'I think I'll give the doctor a call in the morning.'

The next day I phoned the doctor and he said he'd be delighted for some of our fast-growing group to visit the clinic the following Saturday.

'Don't send anyone who is squeamish,' he warned at the conclusion of our conversation.

That Saturday evening we met for prayer as usual at the Mission and then most of the team went out into the pubs and coffee bars. I hand picked a small group of half a dozen to go with me to the clinic.

It was a revelation to talk with the young men who lay on their beds chatting to our team. I saw one heroin addict roll up his sleeve and show the scars made by the needle of death. Christine, the girl talking to him, nearly passed out.

'What's the matter, luv, ain't you ever seen something like that before?' he said, enjoying the reaction he had provoked. Then he added, 'I'm one of the better addicts here. I've only tried to top myself six times.'

At the end of the ninety-minute visit, we went back to the Mission to compare notes. All of us were greatly shocked to see the state of these young people.

'You know,' said Norma, who had gone with us, 'I wonder if God is telling us that we have to do more than just visit them in the clinic. It seems to me that it's no good their going in to be taken off drugs if there is no rehabili-tation for them. Otherwise they just go back to them after they're released.'

'Yes,' I chipped in, 'we need a centre, somewhere we can take them and show them a living faith. But it should be outside of Birmingham, otherwise they'll be tempted to go into the city centre and get more drugs.'

We decided to launch out in faith and I began calling

different people, several of whom suggested I contact a local businessman. He agreed to attend a meeting at our home to discuss plans for our centre. Like all of us, he was surprised when a group of addicts from the clinic also turned up to give us their suggestions.

'They're all as high as kites. Just look at them,' someone remarked.

I had to agree with him. All five of the junkies who had come to 'advise' us sat nodding in their chairs. It soon became evident, as we discussed the urgent situation in Birmingham, that a rehabilitation centre was needed—and urgently.

Days began to turn into weeks since we had that meeting, but no real progress had been made. I was beginning to despair when one day the businessman telephoned.

'Dan, I have just read an advertisement for the sale of a place called Hill Farm in Worcestershire. Could you come and see it with me tonight?'

It took some time to locate Hill Farm, but as we drove around those narrow winding Worcestershire lanes I began to realize that the man was as excited as I was about the possibility of a centre.

'That looks like it,' he shouted, pointing to a farm on the right-hand side of the road. As his car bumped down the farm drive and into the courtyard it became obvious that this collection of semi-derelict buildings had been neglected for a number of years. The house was the only building that looked reasonably sound. The out-buildings looked as if they were about to collapse.

'Nine thousand pounds is the price the agent is asking,' he told me, 'and we need a deposit of nine hundred pounds to secure the farm.' As we walked around the property, dodging the rats, the question kept going around in my mind, 'Is this the place?'

On Sunday morning at the Mission, it was time for me to give out the church announcements. 'If the Lord wants us to have Hill Farm, we will have to hand over the deposit within seven days,' I told the congregation, none of whom had much money in the bank.

Monday morning came and I dashed to the front door. Several letters lay there and I anxiously ripped them open looking for the nine hundred pound cheque. All I found was a one pound note from my Aunt Ethel in Liverpool. 'Thank you, Lord,' I said. 'Only eight hundred and ninety-nine pounds to go.'

As the week progressed, other small amounts came in that totalled about five pounds. But then, on the deadline day, I received a phone call from the businessman, saying that he wanted me to come over to his home as he had some 'interesting news' for me.

His brother was there, too, and the news turned out to be that nearly three thousand pounds had been donated for the purchase of the farm.

'Dan, I think it would be right if you and Norma considered becoming the wardens of Hill Farm,' he said excitedly.

'Don't forget to search him thoroughly,' said the businessman as he handed over Joe, our first visitor to be cared for. Trying to look as if I searched people for drugs every day, I pointed to the bathroom and asked him if he would mind having a bath.

I noticed the blue 'track-marks' on his arms made by many needles.

Joe had a cigarette lighter which I immediately confiscated. 'He's sure to try and smuggle drugs in it,' I told Norma as we both peered at the lighter from every angle. Joe had, by now, finished his bath and was in the bedroom, so I slipped his 'drug-smuggling tool' into my pocket and then locked myself in the bathroom. My fingers shook as I undid the midget screws that held it together. Out came the innards. No drugs in there. I peered into every corner. Still nothing. Very disappointing! Well, all I had to do was to put it back together.

One hour later, almost overcome with steam and embarrassment, I awkwardly handed back to Joe his now dismembered lighter. 'Sorry about that, Joe,' I said in a low voice. 'It isn't quite the same, is it?' He offered me a dry smile but said nothing.

Joe and I soon forged quite a friendship, though his warped obsession with death often disturbed me.

We were shovelling manure in one of the chicken sheds when he first began talking about this obsession. 'I believe, Dan, that one of the most interesting forms of death is suicide,' he said as he bared his snagged, yellowing teeth at me. 'I've tried it five times now. Gassing. Then hanging . . . that didn't work either. Then I slashed my wrists; and I later took a couple of overdoses.'

I wiped the sweat off my face with my arm as my flesh began to crawl. 'But why?' I asked as we continued shovelling and talking.

'I guess all drug addicts often have an urge to destroy themselves. They must have, or they wouldn't use killer drugs.'

Our bizarre conversation was interrupted when Norma called, 'Dinner's ready!' I didn't seem to have much of an appetite.

Soon the addicts were coming thick and fast from the drug clinic after undergoing treatment there to wean them off their drugs.

One of the early arrivals was David, a quietly-spoken young man who seemed an unlikely junkie. He came from a pleasant middle-class home and had loving parents.

Norma perked up when she heard he was a chef.

'You could help me with the cooking,' she laughed.

David was a long-time friend of Joe's and they continued their friendship on the farm. When the work periods had finished, most of the addicts would congregate in Joe's bedroom for a sing-song led by Joe, who enjoyed mimicking Bob Dylan.

Each morning, after breakfast, we would have a short Bible study. While it was optional, most of the lads would stay, although often they were in violent disagreement with what I would say. David rarely said much. I sometimes felt he hid his true personality beneath a veneer of politeness.

Once he did say, 'Dan, since knowing you and Norma, I've changed my ideas about Christianity.'

I wasn't sure whether that was a compliment or not. Then one day he came to me, his face flushed, and said, 'Dan, I think I can make it now. Is it all right if I leave?' With that he smiled shyly. He had been with us a mere three months. Could he survive alone? I had my doubts.

For a while all went well; he travelled around the country, and even lived in Paris for a while. Then he came back to the Midlands. His mother bought him the equipment for a mobile disco and he visited parties around the region under the name of 'Dynamite Dave'.

His mother thought it would be an interest for him, to keep him off drugs. But it did not work. He went back on drugs and was readmitted to the drug clinic. While he was undergoing the treatment, he died. The shock to all of us was indescribable.

I cried when I heard the news. 'Not David. Not lovable, quiet David.'

His friend, Joe, turned to me. His face was deadly pale and his eyes were swimming with tears.

'David was my best friend,' he said, his lips quivering. 'If anyone deserved not to die, it was him.'

But with drugs there is no discrimination.

The sheer mental torment of months of sleeping in derelict houses, and years of alcoholism and drug-addiction, was etched into Bill's pinched, emaciated features. He was in his early thirties, over six feet tall, and his unkempt fuzzy hair, droopy moustache, and wild, bloodshot eyes betrayed his years of pain and neglect.

Bill had come to Hill Farm to get off heroin.

'I want to do a cold turkey,' he insisted, a look of careless abandon sweeping over his face. 'Hospital treatment is too easy.' He had been helped by a Pentecostal Church in Aston which, in turn, had contacted us for help.

I did my customary check on Bill and was horrified to see the state of his body. There were blue scars, slashmarks, track-marks and scabs.

His first night with us went surprisingly well. After a fairly good night's sleep, he spent most of the next morning wandering around the farmhouse wrapped in his scarf and overcoat.

'How are you feeling?' I would ask him periodically. 'Not bad, man. Don't worry. I'll be all right.' As the hours passed and nothing happened, I began to believe that he would come through the 'cold turkey' without any bad reactions.

But then Bill staggered into the kitchen where I was talking to Norma. His eyes had become as large as saucers, and a corner of his mouth was turned down and trembling.

'Dan, I can't go on. Take me to the clinic,' he cried with a look of terror from deep within. 'I thought I could make it, but it's no good.'

I called Terry and Gary, a couple of young volunteers who were helping us, and asked them to sit with Bill as I phoned the businessman at his office.

'Can you come quickly. Bill's in a bad way,' I said urgently. When I returned to the room, Terry and Gary were on their knees praying for him, while his whole body shook and his deep sobs punctured the air.

Then the businessman arrived.

'Okay, Bill. Uncross your legs and sit up.' He laid hands on Bill's head and prayed, 'Oh, God, please help Bill at this time.'

The prayer time continued for at least twenty minutes, then the breakthrough came. Bill stood up and began to smile. The pain was gone and so were the pleas to be taken to the clinic. His physical withdrawal pains had ended as quickly as they had begun.

'God's gone and done a miracle,' he cried through a mist of tears.

11

Trouble Down at the Farm

The only complete catastrophe is the catastrophe from which we learn nothing.

WILLIAM HOCKING

Tensions were building up at the farm as petty squabbles kept breaking out among the addicts. Living in such a closed community, friction was inevitable and soon the farm became a bickering cockpit. Bill would want the radio loud, Joe soft. I would want them to start work, they would want to laze about. Pete, a pill addict, would 'fall ill' and demand I call in the doctor. Others would argue with one of our volunteers, who would accuse them of being a bunch of 'ungrateful layabouts'.

Norma and I were getting desperately tired with all the trouble brewing around us. Then, to make matters worse, the addicts went on strike.

'We want to do something different,' Bill said brusquely. 'It's like a monastery around here. We hardly get any money . . . .' As they poured out their complaints to Norma and me, I could see my wife's face begin to flush with anger. Her working day started at 7 a.m. and often finished well past 10 p.m. Finally, she exploded and tore

89

into them.

'You are the laziest, most ungrateful lot of layabouts I've ever met,' she shouted, her voice rising to an angry tearful shout, her face stamped with harried misery. 'After all we've done for you and now this is how you repay us.'

The lads stood there, mouths open.

I looked at their surprised, hurt and dazed faces. Then I joined in the verbal lashing. I turned my attention to Bill saying, 'I just don't understand you.'

He waited for me to finish and then responded in a voice almost too low to hear, 'I'm not asking you to understand me, man. I gave up trying to do that years ago.' With that he smiled bitterly.

Norma sobbed with emotion that had been building up over a period of weeks, and I took her and Andrew to the nearest bus-stop so she could have a few hours with her mother in Birmingham. Gradually, the lads drifted back to work, but without enthusiasm.

Norma returned that evening and they went out of their way to stop arguing, at least for a few days.

'It was only when you and Norma flipped that we realized the strain you were both under,' said Joe.

But Norma and I knew that we could not carry on for ever under such tremendous pressure.

Norma's face was paper-white except for the dark circles under her eyes. She looked about as sick as a person can get. I could see from her frightened, tear-streaked face as she lay on the bed that she had been crying.

'What's up, darling?' I asked.

'Dan,' she said, 'I've not known how to tell you this, but I'm frightened. A lump has come on my breast.' I guess we both jumped to the conclusion that this was cancer.

It was the last straw. 'Lord, how many last straws are we supposed to have,' I muttered under my breath wondering if this were a bad dream from which I would awaken.

Norma's visit to the doctor confirmed that an immediate operation was necessary.

'We won't know if it is malignant or not until we operate,' he said grimly.

Next day, Joe and Yank, two of the addicts, headed off for a visit to the nearby town of Redditch. Joe had been given permission by a member of the Hill Farm committee to do so, but Yank had not.

Ten o'clock passed and still there was no sign of the pair. Joe had phoned earlier and asked if he could stay out and I had said 'no'.

'Right,' I said to Norma as my nerves cranked up another notch, 'I'll teach them.' I bolted the doors, switched off all the lights and got into bed. I felt so unhappy. Norma was ill, the addicts seemed so unco-operative, and most of the farm committee did not seem to appreciate the tremendous strain we were under.

That night, I asked Norma to read with me a passage that seemed to ask the questions that we were asking in our anguish. It was Psalm 13:1-2:

How long, O Lord? Wilt though forget me for ever? How long wilt thou hide thy face from me? How long must I bear pain in my soul, and have sorrow in my heart all the day? How long shall my enemy be exalted over me?

I felt like screaming out, 'Lord, why have you forgotten us? Why are so many things going wrong for us?'

We both slept fitfully that night and when I woke in the morning I went outside to see if there was any sign of the two. There was, for out of the chicken huts they came, now dishevelled figures.

'Why did you lock the door?' Joe demanded. 'We had to sleep with the chickens.' Not a word of apology from him or Yank.

With this, something just snapped inside of me. All of the emotion that had been gradually building up just burst out. I dashed into the bedroom, lay on my bed and began to cry great, tearing sobs that seemed to be ripping me apart. I felt I was losing the last shreds of my mind.

'I just can't go on,' I said to Norma as she tried to comfort me, the tears coursing down my cheeks. 'I can't handle any more of this. Let's face it, I've made a real mess of this job,' I continued, as my head began to thud. She phoned the businessman and his brother and told them of my condition.

Joe decided he was going to leave and started to pack.

A knock came on my bedroom door. It was a deputation of addicts standing in the doorway.

'Come in, lads,' I said, wiping my eyes and not really wanting to see them.

They stood by my bed and Pete suddenly blurted out, 'Dan, we know you are thinking of leaving, but we want you to stay. We have just said a little prayer for you.'

I burst into tears again. Norma came over to me and held my hand.

'There you are, love, God has heard your prayers. Who would have thought these rogues would have said a little prayer for you?'

They all smiled and Pete ruffled my hair as he left.

But despite that vote of confidence, Norma and I were not sure what we should do regarding our future at the farm. Whether we should stay, or go. Especially with the surgery soon to take place, Norma's health was in question.

So we sought the counsel of one of the farm committee members. After hearing the whole story, he suggested that perhaps it might be better if we resigned.

'You two need a good long rest,' he said.

Norma smiled for the first time in a long while. I soon penned the letter of resignation. Her next smile was two days later when I left the ward of the hospital as she was about to be wheeled into the operating theatre.

I locked the door of our bedroom at the farm and spent a long time on my knees. My prayer time was interrupted by the shrill of the telephone. It was the ward sister from the hospital.

'Mr Wooding, I thought you would like to know that the operation was a complete success. The lump was not malignant!'

At last things were beginning to go right again.

Norma was soon back at Hill Farm, a little shaky, but really looking rested and calm, and looking forward to the prospect that we would soon be leaving and be getting some relief from the turmoil of our time with the addicts.

The furniture van arrived at 8 a.m. on a Saturday morning. It did not take long for the movers to load our furniture and we were ready to set off.

The sad little knot of addicts came and shook hands with us.

'Thanks for everything,' said Pete. 'Don't feel bad about what happened. I know you're both going to make it out there.'

We bumped our way up the farm drive, with little Andrew in the back seat, and moved out into a new life. Soon the new wardens of the farm came to take our place.

Norma and I spent many hours discussing why God had allowed us to go through such a traumatic experience.

'You know, Dan, I think I know why,' she said one day. 'I am sure God has a plan for you to one day help suffering people around the world.'

I was puzzled.

'But how can a nightmare experience like the farm possibly equip me to help others who are going through trouble?'

'Don't you see? Unless you've gone through it yourself, how can you know what they are going through?

'I really believe God can't use you to care for others until you know a little about suffering yourself!'

'But I feel such a failure, love.' I was feeling a great sense of self-loathing.

Norma looked compassionately at me.

'You're supposed to be the veteran Christian of the two of us, but I can tell you that Jesus also appeared to have failed when he was taken and crucified. But look what happened there. That "failure" resulted in the greatest victory the world has ever seen. That same victory can be ours, Dan, if we just allow God to work his way in our lives. You watch. He'll turn this failure into a great victory, too!'

12
It Is Written

He did what he couldn't!
(BROTHER ANDREW'S CHOSEN EPITAPH)

It was hard to summon up any enthusiasm to return to my former job—filing blueprints at a large electrical company in Birmingham. I was the lowest grade clerk of all in that huge office, and for hour after hour I would stand by the dusty files and insert or take out blueprints for colleagues in my department. No one would describe such work as arduous, but I came to regard it as irksome. And my feeling of melancholy was added to by the attitude of my colleagues.

'Looks like you really blew it at that drug farm,' said one of them breaking into peals of insane laughter. (I've always wondered why we British enjoy others' failures more than their successes.)

'We knew you'd come crawling back,' laughed another.

The swiftness with which my world had dissolved and the incomprehensible manner of its going, was a black pool of shadow into which I did not want to look for fear of seeing my own great failure. And the move backwards from being the warden of Europe's first drug rehabilitation farm, to the bottom of the pile in that office, was hard for me to take. It seemed to me that I faced an intolerable web of circumstances.

So, as therapy, I began making notes in my spare time about that traumatic time at Hill Farm and tried to transform these notes into a manuscript. My attempts to reconstruct the whole experience onto blank pages were painfully slow.

'You know, love,' I told Norma one day, 'I have noticed that Jesus and the apostles made constant reference to the written Scriptures. I read recently that "it is written" appears 106 times in the Bible. So the written word is important to God.'

'What are you trying to tell me, Dan?' she asked.

'Well, I'm wondering if God is actually calling me to be a full-time writer.'

Norma looked at me as if I were completely insane.

'I know you have this love for the written word, but you have no qualifications. You failed most of your exams at school, so how could you even get a job?'

I paused and smiled inwardly. 'Darling, my headmistress once told me that I would never succeed at anything in life if I give up at the first hurdle. Later, when I won first prize for the most improved student in the fifth year, she said, "Go after that dream." I plan to do just that.'

My wife leaned over the table and affectionately placed her hand on mine. 'Dan, do it. I'll back you all the way.'

That evening, I went to the file where I kept my Hill Farm papers and I fished out a group of letters from a freelance journalist, Marion Troughton. Marion had sent us a questionnaire at the farm because she wanted to write up a story about our work there. I had answered her questions and she had submitted her story to me and the farm committee for clearance. For some reason, the committee had decided they didn't want the story published and so it never appeared.

I looked at her draft and my answers and marvelled at the way she had skilfully drafted the article together.

I told Norma, 'I wonder if I took that as a model and tried to write a story for a paper, if they would run it.'

Norma knew all about the example of Gideon in the Old Testament who had put forth a fleece to find out God's mind.

'Why don't you write a story and see if it gets published. If it does, you will know it is God's guidance that you should take a step further. You will then begin to discover whether God wants you to become a writer.'

'But,' I said anxiously, 'what can I write about?'

Norma's reply was devastatingly on the mark.

'Why not the Late Night Special that you now help run at Lloyds Bank?'

She was right. Since leaving the farm I had reassumed the leadership of the Messengers from John Miles who had done an excellent job while I was away, and we had linked up with other outreach groups in the city including 'The Ribbons of Faith'. After a period of conducting this evangelistic meeting in the church hall of St Martin's (Birmingham Parish Church) in the Bull Ring, we had taken over an old bank building in New Street and transformed it into a Sunday night coffee-bar. I was chairman of the project.

I persuaded a friend of mine, Dudley Thomas, to take some photographs at the following Sunday's meeting which was aimed at attracting people walking the streets. Then I began putting together a feature on our work.

It was tortuously slow as I typed out the words: 'It is Sunday evening, the time is 9 p.m.; the place, busy New Street, in the heart of England's second city, Birmingham. A hot-dog man is doing a good trade just outside the Lloyds banking hall. He had watched the scores of young people leaving the hall in small teams. They all seemed to have red cards with "Late Night Special" printed on them. A little later they returned with many others with them.'

Not exactly the material to win a journalistic award, but the only way I could test it out was to send it to a newspaper. I had a subscription to *The Christian and Christianity Today,* a London-based weekly which had been taken over from an old-established publisher by the Billy Graham Evangelistic Association. And so I decided to send it to them.

As I sent the envelope containing my copy and Dudley Thomas's pictures, I asked the Lord to show me through the reaction of the paper whether I should continue any further with this apparently lunatic idea of being a writer.

I soon got my answer. For there in the issue of November 10, 1967, was the whole back page carrying the photo-feature. And in the mail that day came a cheque for ten shillings.

I took Norma in my arms and hugged her. 'If I continue in this way and get two million of these published, I could become a millionaire!' I chuckled.

Her eyes were alive with excitement. 'Dan, that's your answer. God wants you to be a writer.'

Soon, I was devoting much of my spare time travelling the Midlands interviewing friends and sending off the results to *The Christian.* It wasn't long before my stories started appearing and I was also pressing on with the manuscript for my book, which I had given the working title of *Junkies Are People, Too.*

The months slipped by, and although the articles were getting into print, I knew I still hadn't got much further in actually securing a full-time job on a paper.

'Dan,' said Norma as I began to exhibit some impatience, 'have patience. We know the Lord wants you to do this work. He will make it clear when you should move.'

The big breakthrough came on May 16, 1968, in a letter from J. Eric Mayer, associate editor of *The Christian.* In it he commissioned me to write a feature on the relationship between blacks and whites in Birmingham's churches.

I jumped up and down with excitement.

'That's just what I've been waiting for,' I shouted to Norma, who was dressing our son, Andrew. 'They have given me a vote of confidence.'

I spent nearly two weeks researching the feature, and then sent it off. Once it was published, I followed up with a letter to the editor, Dr Jim Douglas, asking, 'How about a full-time job?'

The editor was obviously taken aback by my directness, but he did agree to meet me at a writers' conference I was to attend at Hildenborough Hall in Kent. This shy Scot was bowled over by my enthusiasm to be a journalist and invited me to his office in Camden Town to meet Eric Mayer.

The quiet-spoken Irishman didn't seem to mind that I did not have the academic qualifications to be a reporter.

'All I am concerned about, Dan, is can you do the job?' he asked in a no-nonsense voice.

There was an uncomfortable pause as I eyed him across the expanse of his desk, then I replied, 'Well, Mr Mayer, I think you can be the judge of that. You've seen my work and have run all of it.'

He got to his feet and leaned over his desk and shook my hand. 'Congratulations, Dan,' he said in a businesslike voice. 'You've got the job.'

I stumbled out of the office in a happy daze. The salary they were offering was small, but even so I was surprised at Norma's caution when I phoned her.

'Dan, that's wonderful news. But don't you see that we could not live in London on a salary like that. You know we have another child on the way, and that's going to make life even more difficult.'

It was a good job Norma could not see my crestfallen expression. But I knew what she was saying. The cost of living in Birmingham was low compared with London. What should we do about it?

'Norma,' I said as I spoke down the phone, 'do you

believe in that verse which says, "My God shall supply all your needs according to his riches in Christ Jesus"?'

'Of course I do, but we have to be practical.' There was a hint of sadness in her voice.

I brooded over the problem briefly, and then hit on an admirable solution. 'Okay, love, then let's put the Lord to the test. If he really wants me to take this job with *The Christian,* he will have to find us a rent-free home in London.'

A few days later, after a particularly tiring day filing blueprints, my father called me into his lounge.

'Dan, I might have some good news for you.'

'Yes?' I hardly dared to breathe as I waited for him to continue.

'I've heard that there is an old gentleman in Lewisham who is looking for a family to move in with him. They can live in his home rent free if they, in return, agree to take care of him.

'Here's his phone number. Why don't you give him a call?'

I dialled his number and spoke with Percy Crisp, who told me he was chairman of an Eastern European mission.

'Why don't you come and see me?' he suggested. 'We could then see if we would all get on.'

We did and were captivated with his large white house just off Lewisham High Street.

'We'll take it, if you'll have us,' I told Mr Crisp, an elderly man with a sharp, intelligent face and ruddy cheeks.

'I'd be delighted to have you all. I think we'll make a very happy family.'

As we drove back along the M1 to pack up our belongings and move to the capital city, Norma's face was alive with happiness.

'Dan,' she said, 'this is quite amazing. Just a few months ago we were literally kicked off the farm. It just didn't seem to make sense.' She broke into a big smile and added, 'Now God has given you the one thing you've been longing for, the chance to write . . . .'

13

I Have a Dream

I have decided to stick with love. Hate is too great a burden
to bear.

MARTIN LUTHER KING, JR.

My heart began to slam against the walls of my chest as I
entered Shirley House, Camden Road, for my first day as
a journalist. At the age of twenty-eight, I had finally
gained my dream. I was more nervous than a young child
just starting school, and I wasn't sure I was really skilled
enough to work on a national religious newspaper.

But I threw myself into my exciting new job with great
gusto.

One of my first interviews was with Coretta Scott King,
the widow of murdered civil rights campaigner, Dr Martin
Luther King, Jr, who had been brutally gunned down in
Tennessee, just a few agonizing months before.

As I watched her four children scamper around the
house—just like any other children of their age—I
thought of the pain they must all have been through.

I looked at Mrs King and asked if she was worried about
suffering the same fate as her husband.

'I have lived with the threat so long now I hardly think

about it,' she said her eyes ablaze. 'I must do what I must do!'

She glanced across the room at her four children, and added, 'My children are with me in this.'

I thought of her husband's famous 'I have a dream' statement. I, too, had had a dream and it had come true!

Most of my assignments were in London, so I was pleased when Eric asked me if I would go to Blackburn to interview an extraordinary patient there in a mental hospital.

'This man has written a 15,000-word book, yet he can't speak or move his body,' said Eric. 'In fact, he's a spastic.'

As I walked into his ward, I was shocked to see the state of forty-four-year-old Bill Howe. He lay totally immobile in his cot. 'How on earth could he have written a book?' I asked myself in amazement.

I began to talk with the staff and discovered that Bill had been admitted to the hospital as a 'spastic imbecile', which meant, in medical terms, he had an IQ of below forty-five. There did not seem to be much hope for Bill who was constantly ill. The medical report at that time read, 'Concentration nil; unable to reply to anything; no communication.'

Some of the nurses, though, were convinced that Bill was more than just a 'cabbage'. Christian Charge Nurse, Bill Waddington, took the initiative and showed him a three-penny bit and a two-shilling piece and asked him which he would choose. Through grunts and indications in his eyes, he chose the two-shilling piece. With this encouragement that there was life in Bill, Nurse Waddington, along with many others, set out to provide him with the key to a new life—education.

Amazingly, he began to learn. First numbers and then the alphabet. Bill gradually learned to speak—through his left foot. He had a large board with the letters and numbers painted on it at the end of his bed and he would tap them with his foot.

From there he learned to write by lying on his back and painting words with his foot on a stencil. This method proved to be rather slow and laborious so he eventually spelled out the request, 'I would like a typewriter.' The problem was how could he possibly type? This was solved by a shoe for his left foot which was specially made and a wooden peg attached to the sole.

By this method, Bill Howe was able to write his book, *Crossed Wires,* which was published by the Spastics Society in London.

He wrote, 'I found that my brain worked, but not with my limbs. It was like the wires were crossed.'

This amazing author revealed what it was like to be trapped in a body for all those years without any way to communicate with the outside world. He explained how he loved classical music and thought the female nurses were very pretty.

When I returned to London and shared this amazing story with Norma, she said, 'Dan, if it weren't for those dedicated nurses caring for Bill, he would never have learned to "talk" through his feet. They helped a man with no voice to "speak" to the world.'

She fixed her eyes on mine and modulated her voice and I knew that an interesting idea had just occurred to her. 'Have you ever thought that as a journalist you could be used by the Lord to be a voice for those around the world who have no voice?'

She had certainly put a new thought in my mind.

'A voice for the voiceless,' I mused. 'I wonder if it will ever happen?'

As I was becoming more and more engrossed in my work, I felt uneasy about my relationship with David Coomes, the controversial features editor. He had displayed a certain amount of suspicion of me when I first started and he now seemed so aloof and distant. I made a special effort to try and win his friendship. But it was difficult. Then, one day, he confided in me that he had never wanted me to join the staff.

'But why?' I asked, startled at his bluntness.

David seemed embarrassed as he told me of his suspicion of me. 'All I knew of you before you arrived was the weekly bombardment of articles you sent in,' he began, his voice faltering slightly. 'Some were very good, most however were treacly—and I was surprised the editor used so many of them. I was even more surprised when I heard that you were actually joining the paper, and thought it was an unwise step.'

As he saw the hurt in my eyes, he added, 'Time has proved I was wrong—and I don't mean a long time: almost at once you fitted happily into the team. You were a likeable and cheerful friend as well as a colleague, and you were soon writing much "tougher" pieces.'

By that David meant that I was sometimes critical of the events I covered. Up until the event of *The Christian's* pioneering of 'truth before PR' journalism in Britain, each rally was expected to be described as a great success.

But David changed all of that. At the time, he described his distinctive brand of Christian journalism as 'honest journalism', reporting what he saw rather than what others wanted him to see. Some called it 'cynical journalism', hurtful to man and degrading to God.

From joining the staff in 1965 at the age of twenty-two, David tried to avoid the Christian clichés of everything being a blessing and everyone a saint, and told the truth—half-empty halls, few conversions, the ludicrous as well as the blessed, the pathetic as well as the triumphant.

Two things went wrong. Readers fastened on to his critical articles—ignoring his genuine praise for the majority of events and personalities—and unleashed their wrath through some hard-hitting letters.

But worse, David later admitted he did sometimes go too far, substituting personal opinion for fact, cynicism for honesty, and disillusionment for Christian love. Eventually he admitted that he had no defence against some readers' criticisms. 'They were accurate,' he said, his face stamped with pain.

Sitting next to such a person was intimidating, to say the least. Also I could see that a lot of his criticism of big-time evangelism was true. Much of British and American evangelism was like a circus.

My first insight into the problems was when I approached the leader of a certain rally afterwards for a quote.

When I told him the paper I represented, his face became as black as thunder. Then he fixed a reproachful eye on me as if I were an agent of the devil. Eventually he gave me quotes, on condition that I didn't write a critical report.

Then there was a well-known preacher who refused to shake my hand because of my connection with the paper, and Christian leaders who tried to avoid talking to me.

Journalism was turning out to be quite different from what I had imagined. So, to relieve the pressure, I would work on my Hill Farm manuscript in the few spare moments I had. David had agreed to give some editorial input and I had a publisher who had agreed to take it.

But still there was a barrier between David and me. I suppose I was something of an intruder in this strange world of *The Christian*. I knew that much of what was going on was good, stripping away so much hypocrisy, but needles of doubt kept pricking my conscience because I was expected to point out the failings of others, knowing only too well my own.

Our relationship changed dramatically when I was admitted to the Lewisham Hospital with viral pneumonia and was off work for several weeks. David was a constant visitor always bringing with him books and magazines to keep me going, despite the round trip of thirty miles. He was working day and night on the editing of my book, and kept wanting to reassure me of his concern over my illness.

One day he opened up to me about his innermost feelings. 'I think sometimes evangelicals fear the truth,' he said laughing in a nervous, keyed-up way. 'I wonder if their continued existence owes more to half-truth and sleight of hand than to the power of the Holy Spirit. I wonder if potential converts really knew what they were stepping into, whether they would ever dare to take that first faltering step into the kingdom?'

Then he began sharing about the present conflict that was causing us all so much heart-searching on the paper.

'I suppose that working on *The Christian* is showing me that there are Christians who cannot make Christianity work.' His voice was edged with steel.

'I mean, it seems strange that prominent Christians should one moment preach humility, self-effacement, going the extra mile and turning the other cheek, but the next, react violently if an otherwise encouraging news report indicates that they spoke to less than a full house.

'Probably the saddest discovery I have made about some evangelicals is their inability to admit error or to apologize. Is it because by doing so they would imperil God's reputation? I believe the opposite is true. If they did these things—showing humanity and humour in their make-up—then they'd more likely enhance God's reputation as One who deals with ordinary men and not with infallible robots.'

With that he left for his north London home. And I pondered this new way of thinking he had brought my way.

'Dan Wooding, this is your life.' This was a special surprise for me at the Christmas party that Norma and I attended at the office after being away for six long weeks. As I was taken through my short but eventful life, I felt tears brimming at God's goodness to me. I was particularly moved when I discovered that David Coomes had been behind the presentation.

After my 'life' had been well and truly presented to the assembled staff of the Billy Graham office, I was handed the 'This is Your Life' book by David, and then another special package.

'This, Dan,' he explained, 'is your manuscript for *Junkies are People, Too*. I've finished editing it and Val Flint, the editor's secretary, has typed it up for you.'

I felt the tears welling up again. This really was Christian love and concern, and from a man who was supposed to be the most infamous Christian journalist in the country. My tongue was locked.

But problems continued with the paper. David told me that readers, unhappy with our editorial policy, were writing direct to Billy Graham to complain about us all.

I tried to push the feeling of unease away. After all, wasn't this Christmas, a time of goodwill towards all men —even journalists?

14
I Had a Nightmare

I'm going to ask you to get up out of your seats . . . .
BILLY GRAHAM

David Coomes' face was drained of all colour as he put down the telephone and asked me to stop typing my story.

'What's up? You look ill. Is there anything wrong?'

'Yes, Dan, there is! I've just heard that *The Christian* is going to be closed. We're all going to be laid off.'

I stared at him in an almost hypnotic state. How could you close the world's oldest evangelical newspaper just like that? Surely there was a mistake.

'There's no mistake,' he continued. 'Jim Douglas will be calling us into his office in the next few minutes and giving us the news officially. He's absolutely shocked. He never believed the Association would go so far.'

I was indignant. 'I know Dr Graham is used to asking people to get up out of their seats,' I said, trying to cover my shock. 'Now it looks like he's asking us to get up out of our jobs . . . .'

I suddenly felt an overwhelming sense of bewildered desolation at a situation I could not understand.

The closure of *The Christian* was greeted with a storm

of criticism from both inside and outside the evangelical community.

The London *Evening News* headlined the story with '*Billy Graham kills his British paper*'. The article began,

> The 110-year-old weekly *Christian and Christianity Today* is about to be killed. The issue going to press tonight will be the last—a piece of news which the editor, Dr. J.D. Douglas, learned after his staff were told only after last week's issue had been produced.

The British Board of the Billy Graham Evangelistic Association issued a statement in the last issue of the paper expressing 'reluctance and regret'. They said finance was the problem, but we all suspected finance was not the only reason the paper was being axed, and only wished we had been called round a table to discuss problems with the Board.

Letters poured into the office describing the closure as 'murder', 'a disaster for evangelicalism in this country', and 'the heritage of more than a century's Christian journalism has been killed at a stroke'.

The news became a nightmare for me. I was convinced the Lord wanted me to be a journalist and now, less than a year after fulfilling my dream, I was about to be put out on the streets.

David Coomes soon secured a position as features editor on an evening paper in Slough. (In the years ahead he was to edit *The Church of England Newspaper*, then he joined the BBC.) But how could I get a job with my lack of qualifications?

One leading journalist I called for advice said, 'Dan, get out of the evangelical ghetto. There's a great need for Christians to be salt and light in the secular press. I think that's where your future lies.' Then he added, 'I have to warn you that it will be tough. It'll be nothing like working on a Christian paper. It can be a jungle and you may find yourself caught up in many compromising situations.'

That prospect frankly scared me. I knew that working in the cocoon of an evangelical publication was relatively easy. After all, I was surrounded by fellow believers, and I had been told that in the secular media life was quite ruthless. I wasn't sure if I could cope with that—even if I could persuade a paper to take me on.

As I was sitting at my desk contemplating my bleak future, the phone blasted into my thoughts. It was Kevin Murphy, a long-distance swimmer whom I had asked to get in touch with me so that I could interview him about his exploits and how his Christian faith had helped him in his swimming.

'Hi, Kevin,' I said, trying to sound bright, but deep down feeling really depressed. 'I'd love to interview you, but we've been told that we're all fired. So I have no paper to interview you for.'

There was a long silence at the other end of the line as Kevin brooded over the problem. Then he told me something quite unexpected. 'Did you know, Dan, that I am a journalist? I work for a newspaper group in west London that is looking for news staff. 'I know that the *Middlesex County Times,* one of their papers, has a vacancy for a senior reporter right now. Why don't you give the editor, Bert Munday, a call. I'm sure he'd see you.'

I called Norma at our Lewisham home and told her of the news. We had a down-the-line prayer session about it. I knew if I didn't get a job soon, I would have to return to Birmingham and face the crowing of my former colleagues who would rejoice that my dreams had, once again, come crashing down.

'Lord,' Norma prayed, 'we know that with Dan's lack of experience, there is no human way he could get this job. But with you nothing is impossible. So we ask you to work a miracle.'

As I stood across the road from the *Middlesex County Times* in The Mall, Ealing, I became convinced there was no way I could get a position with this historic local newspaper that covered affairs in the huge, multi-racial borough of some 250,000 people. But my former school principal had told me to go after a dream, and so I had asked the Lord to again fulfil that dream even though the odds were stacked against me.

My heart was thumping wildly. 'Pull yourself together,' I muttered to myself. I whispered a quick prayer, then headed across the busy road and into reception. Bert Munday, a tall man from Cornwall, with a shock of pure white hair, put me at ease immediately as I was ushered into his office by his secretary.

I handed him my business card that showed I had been chief reporter with *The Christian*. I didn't tell him, however, that I had been the only reporter, and the rest of the staff had much more important titles. He seemed impressed that he was interviewing a chief reporter, even though I knew that was only a kind title Jim Douglas had given me out of the goodness of his heart.

He studied my card, then he said, 'Dan, did you know that our company printed *The Christian* each week at our Uxbridge printing plant? I used to read it as it came off the line. I thought it was an excellent paper.'

Then he looked directly at me and said, 'When can you start? Today?'

I was staggered.

'Tomorrow, if that's all right with you.' I felt all the breath had been taken out of my body.

Mr Munday smiled and held out his hand to me. 'With your background, Dan, I think we'll start you as a senior reporter.'

It was hugs all round from Norma and Percy Crisp when I brought home the good news that night.

Next morning, I was gripped by a sense of panic. And, as I walked into the office, I asked myself, 'Lord, what am I doing here?' It was less than a year since I left Birmingham, and here I was working on a London paper in an area I knew nothing about. I was in over my head, and I knew it.

I was shown around the office by Mr Munday and found the reporters friendly, but very different from my former colleagues at the Billy Graham office. Smoke curled upwards from several cigarettes, the language was different, and deadlines I was told were of 'vital importance'.

The news editor assumed I knew what I was doing, and immediately assigned me to interview a psychiatrist who specialized in working with drug addicts.

'Go and see what he has to say that might be newsworthy,' he instructed.

I nodded blankly and drove to the address I had been given. The doctor received me warmly, and asked me which paper I represented.

I was shaking with nerves and my mind became a complete blank. 'I'm from the . . . .'

'From where?'

I looked at him desperately, perspiration rising on my upper lip, and waited for him to ask me to lie on the couch and tell him what was wrong.

'Let me take a guess,' he said examining my blood-red face. 'Are you from the *Middlesex County Times?*'

'That's it. You're my first interview.' My nervous silence was followed by nervous laughter.

When I got back to the office I struggled over writing the story. After reading it, the news editor stormed over to my desk and exploded, 'This is awful.' He took a deep drag on his cigarette and snapped. 'Rewrite it with a local angle and a good intro.'

Whispered giggles began to break out from the other reporters in the office. A sick, sinking feeling rose up in my stomach as lazy smoke drifted up from his cigarette to form a haze.

Then he came out with a concept that I've never forgotten.

'Dan, the secret of a good news reporter is the KISS principle.'

'KISS?' I asked hoarsely. I was confused.

'Yes, it means—Keep It Simple, Stupid. Don't try and be clever in your journalism. Just write the story as it is in terms that everyone can understand.'

One of the reporters took pity on me and read through what I had written. He then showed me how to rejig it and make it more interesting.

He looked at my crestfallen expression and advised, 'Dan, a good journalist should never write anything that people can't read during an average visit to the bathroom.' He smiled wryly.

Next day I was assigned to interview Wilfred Brambell, an actor who played the old father in the hit television series *Steptoe and Son.*

Brambell was charming, and I remembered the name of the paper I worked for. However, I reached into my pocket and discovered, to my horror, that I had forgotten my pen.

'Mr Brambell . . . do you think I could borrow your pen?'

What a disastrous start I had made with the paper. And to make it worse, I walked off with the pen.

Fortunately, with the help of the other reporters, I began to gain confidence and write stories that were accepted by the tough news editor. Then Bert Munday decided to back his hunch that I could do the job by giving me a district to work.

'Dan, I want you to cover South Ealing,' he told me. 'I must warn you that it's a difficult patch. We haven't had many stories from there for ages. Just go and make friends with as many people as you can.'

I did, and went from shop to shop, but no one seemed interested in giving me a story. That was, until I reached the Musical Bargain Centre, my last call of a fruitless morning.

'Hi, I'm Uncle Ernie,' said an older man with a Newcastle accent standing behind the counter. 'Would you like some coffee?'

I sat down at the counter in this friendly shop, packed full of musical instruments. Sitting at an electronic organ was a tall, blonde-haired youth, whose long fingers flew across the keyboard. He was making sounds from the organ that I had never heard before.

'Who's he?' I asked Uncle Ernie.

'Oh, a student from the Royal College of Music. His name is Rick Wakeman.'

Soon Wakeman came over and joined us. I told him that I had recently joined the staff of the local paper and was on the lookout for stories.

'I'll give you a good one,' he said brightly. 'I earn a bit of extra money playing as a session musician and I've just played piano on a track for Cat Stevens called "Morning has Broken". It's quite beautiful.

'I also played mellotron on a David Bowie record "Space Oddity", which I think is destined to be a big hit.'

I groped weakly for my notebook and jotted down all that this six-foot-two-inch teenager told me. The result was the first-ever press story on Wakeman, who later went on to play with the group Yes.

Wakeman was right about the Bowie space record and in 1975, on its second release, it was number one in the British charts. And 'Morning has Broken' became a classic.

My friendship with this likeable musician blossomed over the months and years ahead and I eventually wrote his authorized biography, *Rick Wakeman—the Caped Crusader*. We had many opportunities to discuss the Christian faith and he later told me that he had been a Sunday school teacher and had also been baptized.

'Why did you get baptized?' I asked him.

'It was before I started full time in the music business. It was like an insurance policy, a protection against all the nastiness and trouble I feared could happen once I got right into the business.'

I watched in awe as Wakeman moved from being a session musician to a millionaire rock star who owned twenty-one cars, including eight Rolls Royces. I also saw him burn himself out, the result of which was a heart attack at the age of twenty-five. It was sad to witness two of his marriages break up and his finances collapse.

He is now very much in business, still pushing back the frontiers of electronic rock. And he's married again, this time to Birmingham-born model, Nina Carter.

'Hey, Dan, got a moment?' My news editor had the London *Evening Standard* on the line.

'Could you go over to Greenford for them? They've had a tipoff that there has been a bank robbery over there.'

'Sure . . . .'

This was my very first assignment for a Fleet Street newspaper. Soon I was working part time for most of the big papers there, mainly covering robberies, road accidents, court and political stories in Ealing.

'What happens,' the news editor explained one day, 'is that each national and London evening paper appoints a correspondent to cover an area for them. They also appoint a deputy.'

We had left Mr Crisp now and moved to West Ealing, and my name was put forward as an Ealing correspondent for all the papers from the *Daily Mirror* to the *Times*.

Very soon, 'Wooding of Ealing' was leading a very busy life indeed with the local paper work and the Fleet Street assignments. I was working inordinately hard to be as professional as the professionals.

Then Bert Munday called me into his office. 'Dan,' he said holding up the latest issue of the paper which displayed my front-page lead, 'I think you're doing a fine job here. I've decided to make you chief reporter on the paper.' A pleased expression flooded his face.

I tried to speak but nothing came from my mouth.

That night I took Norma out for a celebration Chinese

meal. 'You know, Dan,' she said as she finished her sweet-and-sour pork. 'It's quite incredible what has happened to us over the past few years.

'We've run a drug farm, moved to London and now seen all this happen . . . .' Her eyes sparkled.

'Yes,' I interrupted as I leaned over and kissed her on the cheek, 'it's quite incredible. I've never been so happy in all my life. God has given me the real desire of my heart. I must make sure I never let him down in this work.'

15

Road Block to Moscow

> I took a great dislike to the Dictatorship of the Proletariat,
> and even more, to its imbecilic admirers.
>
> MALCOLM MUGGERIDGE in WINTER IN MOSCOW.

Life on the *County Times* was fascinating. There were
meetings with the mayor at Ealing Town Hall, overnight
assignments in the car park of the police station where a
Palestinian terrorist who had hi-jacked a plane was being
held, and the more mundane duties of covering flower
shows and sports days.

I was busy typing up the results of a school sports day
when the phone rang on my desk.

'Yes,' I said, leaning the receiver on my shoulder and
continuing to pound my manual typewriter.

'Hi,' said the voice at the other end of the line, 'my
name is Ray Barnett. I'm over here from Canada and I'd
like to meet with you later this afternoon to discuss a
proposition. I think you'll be interested in it.'

This Ulster-born Canadian took me to a nearby
hamburger-bar, and as soon as I had ordered my cheese-
burger, got down to business.

'Dan,' he said as I began devouring my food, 'I have

been given your name as a journalist who could well be interested in something I am involved in.'

I said nothing and continued eating.

He leaned over and spoke in confidential tones. 'How would you like to go to Moscow for May Day?'

I stopped eating for a moment. 'Are you joking?' I queried incredulously.

'I'm perfectly serious, Dan.'

It was April, 1973, and Ray's request seemed bizarre to me. After all, I'd never done an overseas assignment and Russia sounded dangerous.

'Look,' said Ray, in his deep Ulster-Canadian accent, 'I run a Christian human rights organization called "Friends in the West". I understand you once worked for *The Christian,* and I thought you might like the challenge of becoming an undercover reporter in the Soviet Union.'

Ray then outlined the daring plan of more than 100 young believers from eight countries who were going to attempt to demonstrate in Red Square on May Day.

'They want to call the world's attention to the Russian Christians who are suffering for Christ,' he continued. 'They also want to let those on the inside know there are Christians in the West who really care for them.'

As we talked, I discovered that the 'invade Red Square' plan had originally been announced by Brother Andrew, the Dutch-born author of *God's Smuggler* and founder of Open Doors, an organization that provides Bibles for Christians in restricted countries. But the volunteers all came from Youth With A Mission (YWAM), an astonishing movement that was founded in 1960 by American, Loren Cunningham, and sends out young people to almost every country of the world.

'Obviously Red Square is going to be the place to be on May Day,' said Ray. 'May Day is the high holy day of communism. Brezhnev and other Soviet leaders will be there to review their troops. And the world's media will be in attendance to cover the event.'

'But,' I asked, scratching my head, 'where do I come in? I'm a small-time reporter on a small-time local paper. Why choose me?'

'Because,' his voice was now excited, 'I believe God told me to approach you to undertake this assignment.'

I couldn't argue with that.

Realizing he had almost hooked me, he went on. 'Before you make up your mind, let me tell you more about the plan. There will be two groups going into Russia, but they will go by two different routes. The first will drive in from England in five mini-buses, the second group of fifty or so, will fly into Moscow from East Berlin.

'There both groups will meet and plan to head for Red Square and hand out St John's gospels taken into Russia by Open Doors. They will wear white paper crosses with slogans in Russian like, "Christ is Risen", "Jesus Loves You" and "Stop Persecuting Soviet Christians".

'My plan is to take in a journalist, and possibly a television newsman, to cover the demonstration from the inside,' he said, watching my eyes grow wide.

'Look, Dan, we can "accidentally-on-purpose" come across the demonstration, film and possibly photograph it, and then get out of the country as quickly as possible . . . if we can! You see, if the demonstrators don't get into Red Square, we can still get the story out. You and I will be right on the spot.'

Ray paused for breath and then asked, 'Would you like another hamburger, Dan?'

Norma sat silently as I outlined the proposition to her. 'Isn't it risky?' she asked, wondering how she would cope if I got arrested. 'After all, the Russians aren't exactly known for their tolerance of demonstrations.'

'There are some dangers involved, but I guess we'll have to trust the Lord to take care of me—and the demonstrators.'

Norma paused briefly and then said uncertainly, 'Okay,

Dan, I'll not stand in your way. If you feel you should go, I hope you enjoy your May Day in Moscow.'

I suppose I was a bit melodramatic, but I wouldn't tell Bert Munday why I needed two weeks' holiday almost immediately. However, he did allow me to place a sealed letter outlining what I was planning to do in the office safe.

'If I'm not back in two weeks, would you please pass this to Bill Molloy, the local MP. He will know what to do if I'm in prison.'

'Prison?'

'I'll tell you when I get back.'

Tony Tew, a BBC film editor and youth leader at St John's Church, West Ealing, which we both attended, agreed to join Ray and me on the trip. Kingsley Fewins, our navigator on the long car trip, was the fourth member of the team. He had a real concern for persecuted believers in the Soviet Union, and took care of visas and ferry tickets from England to Denmark, Sweden and Finland.

In the Finnish capital of Helsinki, we linked up with one of the teams of protesters. The fifty-one-strong group had stopped at a Christian coffee house in the city for a time of prayer and a final briefing before going 'inside'.

It was extremely moving to meet up with these determined young Christians who had all paid their own expenses from countries like the United States, Canada, Australia, Great Britain, New Zealand and the Irish Republic.

After we had cleared all our belongings of anything that would identify us as either Christians or newsmen, Ray shouted over to us, 'Okay, everyone, we're leaving for Russia now.'

We were leaving, he explained, one day ahead of the others. Ray turned to the YWAMers and announced, 'We'll be waiting for you at the motel in Kalinin, which is about 100 miles outside of Moscow.'

He then quietly added, 'Don't forget, when you get there, we don't know each other. I think things will be better if we don't show any recognition.'

With these words, we waved good-bye and drove off in our rented Ford Escort towards the USSR; for some, the most fearsome land in the world.

Driving through Finland's bleak, moon-like terrain, covered with its huge snow-covered rocks and grey shrubs, was an unreal experience for me. I wasn't sure whether I was scared or exhilarated by the prospect of what lay ahead. I suspect it was a combination of both.

Before we knew it, we were at the border crossing. The Iron Curtain was about to part and only a long red-and-white striped barrier barred our way.

A young Russian soldier with a cigarette drooping from his lips came to the left-hand side of the car and demanded, 'Passports.' Somehow his boyish looks and closely-cropped hair made the situation seem less frightening.

But then Tony made a chilling observation. 'Do you see that machine gun he's carrying?' he whispered as we sat in the back of the vehicle.

Our tension mounted as the guard studied our faces and closely examined all of our travel documents. He eventually handed Ray, Kingsley and Tony their passports back. But, without explanation, he held on to mine, turned on his heels and strode into the guardhouse. There he picked up the telephone and held an animated conversation with someone.

'He's probably telling them you're a journalist,' said Ray, his face lined with concern. 'They hate journalists. They'll probably take you, and God only knows what they'll do.'

'Ray . . .' said Kingsley, as the tension mounted in the car.

Just then the soldier came back, his face completely devoid of expression.

'This is it,' I thought.

He saluted, clicked his heels, and handed me my passport. He then ushered us to proceed, manually lifting the barrier.

'Are you ever fortunate!' exclaimed Ray, with mock disappointment in his voice.

Forty suspense-filled minutes after pulling up at the border, we were in Russia. I felt a huge load had been lifted off my shoulders and said to the others, 'Well, chaps, that wasn't so bad after all.'

Kingsley drove gingerly along the winding forest road on the first leg of our 400-mile trip to Kalinin and then on to Moscow.

Just as I was beginning to relax I spotted them . . . three soldiers standing slightly back from the road under the cover of pine trees. As if on command, they sank to their knees and aimed their rifles at us. It seemed like part of a film, but it wasn't. It was real.

'What's happening?' I gasped putting my hand to my mouth. 'Look, those guys are aiming at us.'

Fortunately, Kingsley kept his head and didn't stop. The men relaxed, withdrew their guns, and watched us pass by.

'Welcome to Russia,' said Ray, his face breaking into a huge smile. 'Friendly lot, eh?'

A few hundred yards from the soldiers was a little tree. It was oddly twisted, and huddled under giant firs.

'Look,' said Ray, 'it's grown into the shape of a cross. It's as if the Lord is reassuring us, saying, "Lo, I am with you always."'

Within five minutes, we were out of the forest and had entered a completely barren area. In the distance was a menacing tower.

'This is what is known as "death strip",' explained Ray. 'If you tried to walk across that land you would not survive. It is heavily mined and under close observation by tower guards armed with heavy-calibre machine guns.'

It hadn't struck me at the time, but I had been under the impression that after the initial border crossing all the formalities would be over and we would be free to proceed. I was quite wrong.

The huge clearing we had driven into was a place of bustle, fear, guns and dogs. We pulled up to a huge customs house. A stone tower rose above the trees.

I felt my heart pound as I noticed men in blue overalls going through other cars ahead of us. Each vehicle was driven over a deep pit. A man below, armed with a thin metal rod, carefully prodded every section of the undercarriage, like a dentist searching for cavities.

Another border guard, with a periscopic device, investigated the interior of the petrol tank. The horn button was removed and examined. Door panels were removed.

'Boy, how do the Bible smugglers cope with this sort of thing?' I whispered to Tony as he sat quietly beside me.

Then snarling dogs appeared. They were put into large trucks parked alongside.

'The dogs are sniffing for people,' explained Ray. 'Sometimes drivers will, for a large fee, try to smuggle someone out. As you can see, it's virtually impossible.'

It was then our turn to be searched and we were taken into the customs hall with our bags. Everything, including our wallets, was checked. I noticed one man was checking only for literature.

'They are especially looking for Bibles,' said Ray out of earshot of the guard. 'There's nothing that causes them to froth at the mouth more than the word of God. They really hate it.'

After an overnight stay in beautiful Leningrad, we headed for Kalinin. The main road from Leningrad to Moscow was a pot-holed two-lane affair. We saw the onion-domed churches as we headed towards our destination. They looked beautiful from afar, but close up they were just shells. The front doors were locked tight and the windows were boarded up. We hardly saw one open church on the whole journey.

As we sat at the table of our Kalinin motel eating dinner the next evening with Valentine, our attractive Intourist guide, the other fifty-one weary travellers suddenly appeared in the main dining room, and walked through into another room at the rear. They glanced at us, but showed no recognition.

What we didn't know then was that the KGB were on to their plan—and possibly ours. Some over-enthusiastic Christian in the West had released a story about the planned demonstration and it had been picked up by a local newspaper so the Russians were immediately alerted.

As the fifty-one approached the motel, some of them had been told the trip to Moscow had been cancelled and that instead they would 'tour Kalinin by special bus'. The group were naturally distressed with this news and the tension mounted.

As they were finishing their main course of minute steaks, Viktor, one of the Russian guides, stood up, tapped on a glass with his spoon and asked everyone to give him their attention. His voice had a sharp uncompromising ring.

'I am about to announce our planned schedule for tomorrow,' he said firmly. 'We will have breakfast here in this room at 9 a.m.; take Intourist buses for the tour of the City of Kalinin, and then a boat ride on the Volga River.'

With some of the girls fighting back tears, he added, 'Then we will return to our motel. Thank you very much.'

There was total silence in the room for a few seconds as the impact of the message hit home. Then the shock began to register on their faces.

Viktor tried to explain that there was a problem with their tour vouchers and therefore they couldn't make the planned trip to Moscow for May Day.

Our little group sat quietly listening to the band playing

a mixture of Western and Russian music, when suddenly all fifty-one of the protesters stormed through the main dining room and out into the lobby. The band stopped playing while all eyes were riveted on the group as they marched past.

I heard one of the Americans shout loudly, 'This is ridiculous. We didn't come all the way across Europe to see Kalinin. We are going to Moscow. I don't care what they say. Our vouchers say we can go!'

Anxious discussions were taking place all over the lobby. An Intourist official smoothed back his black hair and said to Ted (the YWAM leader), 'Only those tourists with confirmed accommodation in Moscow can visit the city.'

Ted retorted, 'I don't believe that.'

'There is no room for you in Moscow.'

'Do you mean to say that in your great capital, there is no room for fifty-one people to stand on the pavements?'

Ted went on. 'We are here because we love the Russian people, and we want to be at the May Day festivities. Can't you approve this?'

'We don't have the authority.'

'Who *does* have the authority? Should we call Mr Brezhnev or Mr Kosygin?'

Just then a beaming Ray arrived and pulled me to one side. 'Wow, Dan,' he enthused, 'isn't this exciting? Maybe you could start interviewing people—just in case they get arrested . . . .'

Soon the group occupied the Intourist office. They conducted what would be considered a normal demonstration in the West. Some were singing 'We shall overcome'. I went from one little group to another taking down their names and addresses and getting comments from them about the situation.

Ted was still arguing with the officials. It took all his self-control not to completely lose his temper.

'Most of us,' he said evenly, 'have spent our last penny to make this trip and have gone through much hardship to get here. It would be a tragedy if we couldn't get to Moscow, the one place we have dreamed of seeing.'

After about two hours, a grumpy older man stamped into the motel lobby. He looked irritated at having to leave his home late at night for such a bunch of crazy foreigners. I was called over to this man who turned out to be the local police chief, and was introduced to him by one of the YWAMers.

'See this guy,' he said pointing to me, 'he's a British journalist and he's going to tell the world what has happened here tonight.'

I couldn't believe my ears. Had this person taken leave of his senses? 'I'm supposed to be undercover,' I hissed to him out of the side of my mouth.

By this time Ted and his leaders had agreed on a plan. At 4 a.m. they were going to try to run past the sleeping guards posted at the front door and then drive off towards Moscow in their five mini-buses. But first they needed to get their passports back.

Ted asked for the umpteenth time for them and was again refused by the Intourist chief.

'*Now,*' said Ted, knowing that a lot could take place between then and 4 a.m. At that point, the Intourist boss lost complete control and ordered them out of his office. Each member of the group demanded the right to call his embassy. Someone picked up a phone to get an outside line, but the receiver was snatched back from him.

By that time the police had also arrived and the situation looked very serious. Even so, the young people would not be sidetracked from their demands for their passports.

Finally at 1 a.m. the Intourist boss wearily said something in Russian to one of the guides standing near him. The guide, in turn, spoke, 'Looks like you lot win. You've got your passports.'

They were sternly warned not to attempt to go to Moscow as the consequences would be 'severe'.

Ray took that opportunity to rescue our passports as well, but felt we should not follow on the heels of the group.

'They will definitely be picked up at the first road block and brought back here,' he said sadly. 'If we wait, we'll be able to get the whole story from them and then leave the country as quickly as possible.'

Even as he spoke, a KGB conference was taking place at the motel. They were discussing how to deal with the situation.

The moment of truth came at 4 a.m. The four of us tiptoed down the stairs and hid behind pillars as the group stole down the long, wide staircase, and into the quiet lobby. As they suddenly dashed through the exit, I noticed most of the policemen were snoring in their chairs. Not all of them were asleep, however, and as the group ran for the vans, some of the officers quickly dashed to the phone to raise the alert.

Almost in unison, keys were put into ignitions and the convoy headed in the darkness towards Moscow and . . . trouble!

Police lights flashed, party officials in sombre suits hurriedly jumped out of black sedans, and fifty-one young people milled around the car park of the Tver Motel.

All of the demonstrators were wearing white crosses around their necks with slogans in Russian like 'Christ is Risen' and 'Stop Persecuting Russian Christians'.

Valentine, who was sitting with us at the breakfast table, shook her head in disbelief. 'But,' she said, 'they cannot demonstrate like this in Russia. Do they not understand this?'

We all looked suitably shocked, excused ourselves, and proceeded to the lobby to talk with the demonstrators.

'Have you seen what's going on outside?' One of them asked me. 'Just take a look.'

I stepped outside into the freezing morning air and was

greeted by a sight that chilled me to the bone. There, surrounding the motel, were about fifty uniformed figures all clutching rifles.

Gradually, we were able to piece together the story of what had happened to the group. After about eighteen miles they were faced with the impasse that Ray had predicted.

Nick Savoca, one of the group, described what happened in his book *Road Block to Moscow,* written with Dick Schneider (Bethany Fellowship):

> Far down the highway sat a giant truck-trailer parked directly across it. One lane was open but blocking it was the black sedan we had just seen. Beside the highway loomed a checkpoint tower.
>
> Even from here we could see the police van and its base and the armed figures standing around it.
>
> It was a full-fledged roadblock.
>
> I knew it was ridiculous, but I frantically searched for escape routes leading off the highway. But the highway led us relentlessly to the roadblock.

As Ted tried to explain to the police that their visas were approved for Moscow, the situation became even more tense. For fifteen minutes the group sat there praying. Meanwhile, the police stood resolute.

> Brakes squealed behind us and we looked out to see another sedan drive up. The door swung open and out stepped Andre, our old acquaintance from Kalinin.
>
> He stood on the highway casting a long shadow behind him from the new sun. He lit a cigarette, drew on it, and exhaled the smoke as he looked at us.
>
> Ted opened the door of his van and stepped out. I followed him along with Tony, Ralph, and a few other kids. We walked up to Andre.
>
> He dropped his cigarette on the pavement, ground it with his heel. 'I suppose by now you are very sick of me,' he said wearily, 'but you will not be allowed to go to Moscow.'

It was by that time nearly 7 a.m., almost two hours since

they had been halted at the road block. They were now surrounded by some thirty police and KGB men. The protesters in the vans were quietly watching the little group as they stood in confrontation with the symbols of Russian power.

Savoca looked at Ted. He could see Ted was weighing something in his mind and struggling to come to a decision.

'I knew he was praying and seeking guidance,' said Savoca. 'His answer wasn't long in coming.

Ted turned to the kids in the vans. 'All right,' he announced loud and clear. 'We are not going to be allowed to go farther than here.' He waited for a moment, then continued. 'I have the guidance,' he stated, 'that we should preach the Gospel of Jesus Christ to these people right here and now.'

Savoca said an electrifying thrill shot through him. And a unanimous roar of 'Praise God!' resounded from the vans. They could again openly be Christians. The group tumbled out of the vans carrying their large paper crosses. He continued:

Many held them high in the air as if they were flaming torches, others put them around their necks. And then, all fifty-one of us standing together, raised our hands to heaven, looked up and began singing lustily, 'Hallelujah, for the Lord our God, the Almighty reigns . . . .'

The group stood there beside the highway and continued singing and chanting, 'Christ is risen!' and 'Jesus loves you!' in Russian. More police vehicles arrived and now a large number of police and security officers stood before the protesters. They were stone-faced as the group told them in Russian, 'We love you . . . we love you.'

As some snickered or stared sardonically, one policeman strode up to them as they were standing in line and singing and took close-up, head-and-shoulder pictures of each of them.

Savoca asked Andre, who had since returned to their

group, 'Why does your government persecute the Christians so?'

'Persecute them,' he snapped, flicking away his cigarette butt. 'That's what *you* say.'

'But we have reports,' said Tony, one of the group.

'False,' snorted Andre, 'propaganda from troublemakers.'

'Then what is *this?*' Savoca handed him a list of names of Russian Christians now serving prison sentences for their belief. One of the group had smuggled it in under a shoe innersole.

Andre studied the list, but said nothing. Then one of the policeman took it, looked at it, and passed it to another. One pointed to a name as if he knew the prisoner.

After two hectic hours of protesting and witnessing, it became apparent that they were all under arrest. The group was completely hemmed in by police cars, vans and trucks.

Ray, Tony, Kingsley and I, all began to register our protests at being held under 'house arrest' with the fifty-one YWAMers. The Intourist staff, having all got king-sized headaches by now, finally backed off and said, 'Your group can leave, not the others. But you must not go to Moscow. We will give you a police escort part of the way back to make sure that you do not take the *wrong* road . . . .'

We quickly told our friends that we had persuaded the Russians that we were not part of the demonstration and were off to publicize the story. They hastily gathered up film that had been taken of the road block protest and we did our best to conceal the film in our belongings and in the car.

After an overnight stay in Leningrad, we headed for the Finnish border. I found the situation even more tense leaving the Soviet Union than it had been going in. We thought that our films would surely be found and confiscated. The hold-up at the first border check seemed longer than before, and the guards appeared even more menacing.

At the customs building, they thoroughly examined all our belongings. After about an hour of the various checks, we were told to proceed to the final border post. Even that drive wasn't without its drama. As we headed off in the car, we heard a dreadful screeching sound under the car. Something had become lodged underneath and we were afraid sparks might cause the car to catch fire.

'Just keep going,' Ray urged Kingsley. 'It's a choice between possibly being sizzled alive or stopping and being shot.'

We just made it. As the border guard checked our passports, Tony looked underneath the car and found a huge piece of twisted wire that had become lodged.

As the red-and-white border pike was raised, we all offered thanks to God for getting us out safely. We also prayed for the group we had to leave behind.

Just past the Finnish checkpoint was a cafe and I began drafting the story on a napkin. Then I called the London *Evening News,* and a friend whom I had briefed about the trip put me through to one of the copy-takers. He thought I was playing a practical joke when I said, 'It's Wooding of Ealing calling from Finland,' for up until then, I had only done local stories.

'Are you drunk, old boy?' he asked.

'No, certainly not. I'm phoning from Finland. Look, would you please take the story.'

He paused and I heard him say to a colleague, 'It's Wooding of Ealing. He thinks he's phoning from Finland. I wish these guys wouldn't start drinking so early in the day.'

After he finally took the story, I called Associated Press and United Press International in Helsinki and gave it to them also. Neither one had heard a word of the incident.

'The problem,' one reporter told me, 'is that Moscow correspondents need two days' written permission to go outside a forty-mile radius of the city.' So they would not have heard about this.

The Soviet authorities finally decided to kick the fifty-one YWAMers out of the country, and a police escort accompanied them the entire 400 miles to the border.

When they arrived in Holland they were greeted by Brother Andrew. He filled them in on what had happened to the other group that had flown direct to Moscow. Most of them had been confined to their hotels on May Day.

'The Russians told them they had been alerted that a group of Christian radicals were coming to stage a demonstration. Therefore, they couldn't allow anyone out of the hotel.'

Brother Andrew revealed, however, that sixteen of the young people did get out of the hotel and witnessed in a park. But they were promptly arrested and expelled.

'It was obvious the Russian government had received word of your trip and were afraid,' said Brother Andrew. He explained that the gospels of John which had been smuggled into Russia for them to distribute on May Day were in good hands.

'The Russian Christians will hand them out instead,' he said, "and this, too, will be very effective. I feel the Russian Christians were greatly encouraged by your outreach. Not everybody was for it. But many in the unregistered church were enthusiastic.'

After such a trip, it was hard to settle back into life in the small newspaper office. Reporters that Monday morning were being dispatched to cover the local court, or to follow the mayor around on his duties.

'Dan, it's good to have you back,' said the news editor. 'Did you have a nice holiday? Well, anyway,' he continued, 'there's a really nice sports day I'd like you to pop along to cover later today. See if you can get a good human interest angle out of it . . . .'

16

From Saigon with Love

History teaches us that when a barbarian race confronts a
sleeping culture, the barbarian always wins.

ARNOLD TOYNBEE

The trip to Russia caused quite a stir locally and I received
several invitations to speak at different functions. After
telling members of Ealing Rotary Club about the eventful
trip, I was approached by a senior member.

'Dan, would you be free to go on a tour of the Far East
for the London Rotary Clubs?' he asked casually. I was
stunned.

'Are you joking?' I asked, feeling I had been awakened
from a deep dream.

'No, I'm deadly serious. Our London district is sponsor-
ing what is called a Group Study Exchange with our
Southeast Asia region. I'd like to nominate you to go as
part of our educational and cultural team.'

Things moved very quickly and on a cold February day
in 1974, I joined a team of young London professionals
and Alan Bruce, our team leader, for two incredible
months of travelling throughout that fascinating and
shocking part of the world.

135

It didn't take long after our arrival at Calcutta's Dum Dum airport to be launched into the poverty that is India. A little boy stumped up to me swaying his tiny body from side to side. He was legless and was using his hands to propel himself forward. He could not have been more than six years of age, yet was already a seasoned (and scarred) fund collector in a relentless life-and-death battle for food.

He sat upright on his stumps and held out his hand pointing to his mouth. His eyes were glazed and I thought of Peter, my six-year-old son, in England. How could I refuse him? I gave him a rupee and then, with my colleagues, set off in a taxi into the festering, foundering metropolis where hundreds of thousands of sick, starving human beings live a lingering death in the gutter.

The sights I encountered in Calcutta will remain with me for the rest of my life. Cows were everywhere. They were asleep on the pavements and in the roads, possibly reflecting on the good fortune of being sacred in a world where Philistines everywhere else ate their unfortunate relatives.

In the city, my heart went out to the barefoot children who trailed after us asking for money and not accepting 'no' for an answer. They padded along, touching my arm and pointing to their mouths. Whole families lay on filthy pavements outside decaying buildings which once housed the British. Babies suckled vainly at dry breasts after being born in the dust days before.

Our team stood stunned as we watched Mother Theresa's Sisters of Charity fight to stem the advancing tide of disease and hunger. They doled out soup and bread to the endless line of starving people at one centre. We saw one of their trucks setting off with a cargo of food for a leper colony.

We toured a home for abandoned children and saw cots containing tiny helpless babies found in gutters, alleyways, or simply handed in by desperate mothers who couldn't cope with yet another mouth to feed.

As I tried to comprehend the misery, I wondered how such a situation could be allowed to exist.

'Why do you do this work?' I asked one of Mother Theresa's nuns, who came from Ireland.

'We do it for God. We are told in the Bible that if we even give a cup of cold water to one of his children, we are doing it for him.'

These selfless people were a great challenge to my faith as a Christian. I had never seen such life and death situations before.

After a short spell in India, we moved on to Singapore where we addressed several Rotary Clubs and were shown around this city-state which has one of the highest standards of living in the far East.

From Singapore we went to Malaysia and then across to Sarawak, Sabah, and Brunei in Borneo. We arrived in Bangkok, Thailand, where the *Bangkok Post* called us the 'emissaries of goodwill'.

There came a possibility of finishing our tour in South Vietnam but, not surprisingly, I found that the rest of the team didn't feel too happy about going on to Saigon, so I made the decision to go there on my own.

'A Dr Wang will meet you at the airport,' I was told by our leader, Alan Bruce. 'He is a leading Rotarian in Saigon.'

I don't think I had ever prayed so much as when our plane flew over Vietnam. As I looked down, I felt terror as I saw hundreds of bomb craters pock-marking the whole countryside. This indeed was a country scarred by a terrible war.

At the time, the Americans had withdrawn their 500,000-strong army and, despite the so-called peace agreement with Ho Chi Min, the Viet Cong were continuing their inevitable push towards Saigon.

'I am surprised a journalist would come here now,' said the passport control officer at the heavily-guarded Saigon

International Airport. 'We are facing a nightmare, yet the world's press largely ignores our plight.'

He smiled as he handed my passport back to me. 'Have a good stay in my country,' he said, adding, 'And write the truth!'

I thanked him and headed out through the barrier. I looked in vain for the doctor, but he was not there. My heart was now pounding violently. What should I do? I was in a strange and dangerous country. And all I had with me was a piece of paper with his name and phone number on it.

A kindly airline girl agreed to phone through to him and discovered he was dealing with patients. Apparently he had been given the wrong flight to meet, and had returned to his surgery thinking that I had decided not to come after all.

'He wants you to take a taxi to this address,' she told me.

After passing through the various airport road blocks, we were soon tangled up in a mess of bicycles and mopeds that were clogging up the road. There were also many horse-drawn carts, now back in favour in this war-torn land. We passed two men who were fighting at the side of the road. It was a violent scrap with fists and feet being used equally.

'You Yankee?' asked the driver.

'No, I'm English,' I responded.

His face lit up. 'I'm glad. Yankees gone and ditched us. They said they were our friends, then they left.'

His face became very serious.

'You tell the people in your country that we will fight to the death. But still the VC will win.'

Soon we pulled up outside a large house surrounded by a high wall. The driver honked his horn and a girl suddenly opened the gate and let us in.

'Is Dr Wang in?' I asked.

She bowed.

'He at work. But wife is here.'

As I went into the house, I was greeted by Mrs Wang, a slight Chinese lady.

'You are welcome in our home. Thank you for coming. Not many people do these days.'

After Chinese tea and polite conversation, Dr Wang arrived.

'Mr Wooding, I can't thank you enough for coming to Saigon. You will get a deep insight into the real truth about what is happening here.'

As the portions of the Chinese meal were served to us, the stocky doctor told me his story.

'My wife and I came here from Shanghai about twenty-five years ago when I was a newly-qualified doctor. I was really shocked when I saw the plight of the thousands of poor people living here. So we both decided to settle. Since then I have treated more than a million Vietnamese free of charge.'

I gasped.

'Do you know that in our war-torn land we now have about 400,000 war orphans?'

When I was shown to my bedroom on the second floor, Dr Wang informed me that the room had been taken over by the Army during the Tet Offensive, when the Viet Cong had tried to take over Saigon.

'There were gun battles going on from your balcony,' he said in a matter-of-fact way.

Having never been in a war zone before, I was finding the tension difficult to cope with.

Next morning I wanted to take some photographs of Dr Wang's Rotary Clinic for children, which was across the road from his home. As I pointed my camera and pushed the shutter, an arm came around my neck and began throttling me.

'Argh . . . .' I made a sharp glottal sound of surprise.

I could feel myself losing consciousness as I fell back-wards.

Then I heard Dr Wang's angry voice shouting at my assailant.

'Let him go,' he yelled loudly, his eyes bulging with fury. 'He's with me.'

The man eventually let go of my throat and I got up from the ground and looked up at a young man with a terrible scar across his face.

'I am sorry for that Mr Wooding,' said the doctor. 'He thought you were photographing the machine-gun post in front of the clinic. Men who have been injured in battle, like this one, are stationed to watch for suspicious characters who try and photograph military installations. If I were you, I'd be a bit more careful with that camera.'

As I sat with him during his surgery and saw the never-ending stream of youngsters, he turned to me and said, 'My philosophy is simple. To safeguard children is to safeguard humanity.'

After I spoke at Saigon Rotary Club, Dr Wang arranged for me to visit a refugee camp well outside of Saigon. It took a special pass to get there through the various road blocks and a driver and guide were arranged for me.

When we arrived at the Camp—a few corrugated iron huts on a desolate piece of ground—I was taken to the main gate where a couple of soldiers were jabbering away in Vietnamese on walkie-talkie radios. They examined my documents and then ordered me to follow them. Suddenly I was being held in a hut and the men were now shouting at each other in an excited way.

I looked desperately to my guide for an explanation.

'They think you are a Viet Cong spy.' A jittery smile hung on her face.

I utttered a shaky little laugh.

'I don't know,' I thought to myself. 'The Russians hold me and now these people think I'm on the opposite side. The world's absolutely crazy.'

The guide was deeply embarrassed.

'It seems that your papers are not completely in order and everyone is very jumpy these days about the VC.'

Eventually, I was ordered at rifle-point to reboard the mini-bus to Saigon.

'Mr Wooding,' she said gently, 'you will be pleased that they now say they believe you are not a spy, but you cannot look around the camp until you get the proper documentation.'

Next day, I was able to get the right papers and went back, this time to be treated as a VIP. I was able to interview whomever I wished and to take as many photographs as I wanted.

Each day in Saigon I met heroes. Relief workers, medical staff, missionaries, all who would not leave their posts of duty.

'We know we could be killed, but we will not leave,' said one American missionary. 'God has called me to Vietnam and here I will stay—to the very end!'

When the time came for me to leave Saigon, I had tears in my eyes. I thanked the doctor and his wife for their kindness to me during my stay.

'My eyes have been opened by this visit,' I told them. 'Anytime you're in England, I would be honoured if you would come and stay with Norma and me.'

Doctor Wang and his wife looked as if they had been through a nightmare when they arrived at Heathrow Airport. It was just one year since I had been with them, and Vietnam had fallen to the Communists. The couple, who had dedicated a quarter of a century to serving the people there, had been forced to flee for their lives. The country was in turmoil.

'We lost almost everything,' said Dr Wang after I had introduced him to my wife. 'We are going to have to start our lives again from the beginning.'

The couple did stay with us for a time in our new home in Walton-on-Thames and became valued members of our family. Then I discovered that some of Dr Wang's former patients were in England at the Ockenden Venture Home in Haslemere. The orphans had been flown over to England by a newspaper that had mounted a last-ditch effort to 'rescue' the children from the mayhem that was expected to result from the fall of Saigon.

The paper had prominently featured the airlift, but had come in for considerable criticism for taking the children out of their natural environment, however bad it had been.

But I was still shocked with the apparent callousness of the man on the picture desk when I told him of this reunion between Dr Wang and their 'war orphans'.

'We've gone off Vietnamese war orphans, old boy,' he said curtly. 'Sorry, we're not interested.'

'But you brought them over . . . .'

With that the phone went dead.

The good doctor and his wife have now started their lives again in another part of the world, and when I saw them off at Heathrow Airport, I suddenly felt ashamed of part of my profession. For the words of that man on the picture desk kept repeating in my mind.

'We've gone off Vietnamese war orphans, old boy.'

Then I thought of the words of Jesus: 'As much as you do it unto these children, you do it unto me.'

17

A Tale of Two Prisons

Remember those in prison as if bound with them.

THE APOSTLE PAUL

The phone shrilled on my desk at the *Middlesex County Times*. It was the cultured voice of a local clergyman who had allowed me to write up a story of his friendship with Britain's most notorious gangsters, the Kray brothers— Ronald, Reggie and Charlie—who were all currently in prison for their misdeeds.

'Dan, I've just had a call from Violet, the boys' mother,' he said in his rich accent. 'She likes your article and wants to invite you for tea.'

I was dumbfounded. 'But isn't that dangerous?'

'No, not at all,' he said confidently. 'She's a lovely lady. Don't believe all you read in the papers.' I heard him chuckle on the other end of the line.

Sitting in the small office with me was Mike Watson, the sub editor. He could see the colour had drained from my face. 'What's up, Dan?' he asked. 'You look as if you've had a nasty shock.'

'I have,' I said quietly. 'Violet Kray has asked me round for tea! Do you want to join me? I think I need some

143

moral support.'

I had read so much about this family; how they were said to have controlled London's underworld and were blamed for many shocking acts. So tea with the matriarch of the Kray family, whose name was synonymous with violence, was an intriguing and frightening prospect.

My heart was pounding unmercifully as Violet, an open-faced strawberry blonde, opened the door of their London flat and welcomed us inside. Both she and her husband, Charles, a small, thin-faced man, made Mike and me feel at home in the place where twins Ronald and Reggie had been arrested by the police.

Their living room was comfortable, and all over it was evidence of the boys' regard and affection for their mother. Hanging on one wall was a painting of a cottage surrounded by green fields. It was Ronnie's first painting with oils. His studio was a cell in Her Majesty's Prison, Parkhurst, on the Isle of Wight. On another wall was a British Amateur Weightlifting Association certificate presented to Reg for his weighty exploits in the prison. Dotted around the room were also brightly coloured, beautifully-made teddy bears and other soft toys. Ronnie and Reggie had made them as presents for their mother.

There was a haunting sadness in Violet Kray's eyes when she said in a barely audible voice, 'I can't tell you how much I miss the boys. They were everything to me.'

Then she locked her confused eyes on mine. 'Dan, I enjoyed reading your story in the Ealing paper. Ronnie has read it and I have a little note for you from him.'

It was handwritten on toilet paper and on it Kray 'suggested' that I should write a book called 'Kray Country' which was to be for 'propaganda purposes'. It would, he said, be full of quotations and stories 'from celebrities who have met us and know us well'. There followed a list of top British show business and political personalities which read like a *Who's Who*. I could hardly believe that this man, who some had called Britain's Al Capone, was giving me a 'request' I could hardly refuse.

I looked desperately at Mike for moral support. He appeared to be as embarrassed as I. After another cup of tea, we left. Violet saw us into the graffiti-marked lift, and I heaved a sigh of relief as the doors squeaked close.

'Well,' I said to my companion as we headed for the ground floor, 'there's a turn-up for you. How am I going to get out of this one?'

Mike smiled faintly and said nothing.

Then came an invitation from Reggie Kray for me to visit him and his twin brother in Parkhurst. I also received a letter from the Prison Governor saying that if I wished to be placed on the approved list of visitors I would need to fill in the form that was enclosed and also send two passport-type photographs. Shortly after this, a police officer appeared at my home to 'check me out'.

When he discovered that I was a journalist and that I hadn't known the twins before their imprisonment, he told me he didn't hold out much hope that I would be allowed to visit Reggie.

He was right! I received a letter from the Governor saying that he had received instructions from the Home Office 'to the effect the regulations do not permit your name to be included as an approved visitor or correspondent to 058111 Kray'.

A huge relief flooded over me. I was frankly quite scared to visit this infamous pair, but still Violet kept in contact and urged me not to give up on the book project. I mentioned the idea to a Fleet Street contact on the *Sunday People* and he suggested that they could be interested in a special series on the life of the Krays behind bars.

Although I was not an 'approved . . . correspondent' with the Krays, I began writing to them regularly and receiving their replies. It was fascinating to be conducting correspondence with these two men who wrote to me as if I were an old friend. None of the letters were ever stopped by the authorities, so I just kept writing.

The newspaper was, by now, pressing for as much material as I could muster, and so I began to write out lists of questions for the twins, and Violet would smuggle them into Parkhurst for me. The following week she would bring out the hand-written replies, usually from Reggie.

He wrote on one occasion from his cell in the Maximum Security block:

> It's a sanctuary for me, just like one's own bedroom outside. That's why I don't like other people in my cell. It's cozy with a writing desk, a toilet stand, two other tables as well, with my record player and radio on them. There's a photo of Mum on my desk, a photo of my girl Christine on the other table, and one of Frances, my late wife, and myself, on the wall. The bed has a flowered cover on it.
>
> There's a calendar on the wall, sent by a friend with these words—which seem appropriate for one in my predicament:
>> Oh Lord, grant me the serenity to accept
>> the things I cannot change;
>> The courage to change the things I can
>> And the wisdom to know the difference.

Through Violet I was able to send in Christian books, a copy of the *Living Bible* and many Christian records, all of which were gratefully received by the twins.

As I began to research the feature, I was introduced to many friends of the Krays. And Violet would let me drive her around the ugly streets of London's East End, where the family had lived for most of their lives. Many of the terraced houses there had been demolished to be replaced by groups of grotesque high-rise concrete cell blocks. It was Moscow come alive in the city where Karl Marx toiled for years with his 'twenty-six lead soldiers'.

I noticed the pub which looms large in Kray folklore, the 'Blind Beggar,' where Ronnie is said to have coldly shot gangster George Cornell, a member of the rival Richardson gang, and then walked out, banking that the East End would not talk. But it did!

'Turn left past the Blind Beggar and that will bring you into Vallance Road where we used to live,' Violet told me.

For a few brief moments I was taken back a generation as we toured the little cobbled back streets of Bethnal Green. As my car moved at walking pace, the motor whining in first gear, I saw the pub where Violet used to be a regular; the corner shops where she and the boys shopped, the park where the twins played as children and the cafe they used as the headquarters for their early villainy. The 'two-up two-down' terraced houses no longer stand there, having been replaced by a few corrugated iron fences hiding a site later to be built upon.

As I stopped my car, she pointed to the spot where police cars would park twenty-four hours a day.

'They used to sit there watching who went in and out of our house,' she said with a face white and strained. 'Ronnie would feel sorry for them and one night said to me, "Mum, I think they must be hungry and thirsty sitting out there in the cold. Do us a tray of tea and biscuits and I'll take it out to them."

'They were most grateful. One of them brought it back a little later and thanked Ronnie very much.'

But now, because of their crimes, they had, in Orwell's parlance, become un-persons.

Soon I was to meet one of the Kray brothers. The eldest, Charlie, was to be allowed out of prison for a spell of acclimatization before possibly being freed. He was not thought to have played such a serious role in the crimes attributed to the twins.

The *Sunday People* asked me if I would try and gate-crash his welcome-home party, but that wasn't necessary as I phoned Violet, and she said I could come as a special guest.

One day Ronnie wrote and said he had been delighted to read of a kind remark about the twins in a book, *For Adults Only*, by Diana Dors. I phoned Diana with the news and she suggested that I take her and her husband Alan Lake over to see Violet, her husband Charles, and Charlie, who had been released from prison. With a delicious sense of voyeurism I watched the discussion unfold as many fascinating stories were relived.

When the articles appeared under my by-line in the *Sunday People,* several members of the Kray family and their friends made it clear to me in no uncertain way that they were not pleased with some of the material. For a time I became very concerned for the safety of my family and myself. After all, you didn't mess with the Krays. Fortunately, nothing happened to us.

I felt a flush of sheer excitement as I stepped off the Ethiopian Airlines plane at Lagos Airport and into the sauna-like heat of West Africa in the summer of 1976. At last I was back in Nigeria, the country of my birth. I had been in Kenya for an American relief agency and they had asked me to go on to Nigeria to cover another aspect of their work.

'I'm here to discover my roots,' I grinned to the Englishman who waited in line with me for the immigration officer to check our passports. 'I've always wanted to return here.'

My travelling companion presented his passport and was waved through.

'See you on the other side,' he mouthed as he disappeared into customs.

I smiled warmly at the official as he began studying my travel document.

'Where's your visa?' he snapped in a most unfriendly fashion.

'Visa?' I asked. 'Why do I need a visa? I was born here.'

'Are you a Nigerian citizen?' he asked in rapid-fire fashion, his eyes throwing off sparks.

'No, but . . .' My cheeks turned to bright crimson.

'You will pick up your baggage and follow me.'

In a state of shock, I staggered under the weight of my
baggage, struggling to keep up with the striding official as
we wove our way through the crowds milling about. Obviously, I thought, we were going to have a cup of tea and
rationally discuss this problem.

He stopped suddenly outside a door marked 'Detention
Cell.' He unlocked the door and said, 'You will stay in
there until we decide what to do with you.' With that, he
got behind me and gave me an unceremonious push into
the cell which already held four African prisoners. I stood
there frozen with shock for a moment, not totally comprehending what was happening to me. It had all taken place
so quickly that I had had no time to react.

Then I noticed that one of the Africans was on his knees
on a straw mat praying towards Mecca. He stopped suddenly and gazed at me in shocked disbelief. The others
stopped their babble of conversation and sat staring at me.

'Err . . . I'm Dan Wooding from England,' I stammered. Then, as a reflex action, I reached into my top
pocket and brought out my business cards and handed one
to each of them.

The Africans looked at them in bewilderment and then
gathered around me. 'What have you done?' asked one.

'I don't know. I think it's because I haven't got a visa.'

Two of them explained they were from Senegal, the
others from Mali. They told me they had also arrived
without visas.

'We are starving. They have given us no food or drink
for two days,' said the man who had by now given up
praying to Allah. 'I'm trying to sell my sewing machine to
pay for my fare out.' He faced me square on. 'Would you
like to buy it? It's a Singer, you know.'

I looked at the sturdy, black machine with its familiar
trademark and tried to explain that I hadn't much use for
a sewing machine at that very moment.

In blind frustration, I began banging on the door and
demanding to be allowed to speak to the British Embassy

in Lagos. There was no reply, so I angrily wrote a note which read, 'I demand to know why I am being treated like a dog,' and slipped it under the door of the cell.

It was quickly picked up by the guard who read it and then shouted, 'Shut up, white man. Otherwise you'll be in even more trouble.' I suddenly felt a growing terror as I knew that this was no idle threat. I had read the press stories of executions being carried out on Nigerian beaches and soccer stadiums, and being transmitted live on television. My flesh began to crawl as I realized the serious situation I was in.

I noticed there were only four bunk beds in the cell and there were five of us. One of the Africans read my mind and pointed to the bed he had been lying on.

'Take it,' he said kindly as he fingered his prayer beads. 'I will sleep with my brother.'

It was now dark outside and the stark, bare light bulb that glared from the ceiling cast strange shadows around the room. In the office next door I could hear the guards shouting and laughing. They were speaking in the Hausa language, so I couldn't understand what they were saying, but that made their echoing conversation seem even more ominous to me.

The heat in that tiny room was stifling and my throat tightened. I began to shake with a combination of fever and fear.

I looked at my fellow prisoners. They were of a different faith, yet appeared to be taking the situation much better than I. I felt a great shame at that moment.

I managed to find my Bible in my suitcase and asked them if they would mind if I read it. 'You see,' I explained, 'I'm a Christian so we're all people of "the book."'

They nodded. I fluttered the pages of my Bible and found myself reading passages from Matthew and finally my eyes settled on chapter 25:36, 'I was sick, and ye visited me: I was in prison, and ye came unto me' (AV).

'Lord,' I prayed silently, 'I really need you to visit me at this time. I'm scared, really scared.' I felt a choking sensation in the base of my throat, and the sharp sting of tears.

All of a sudden the fear melted away and I felt an all-enveloping peace come over my whole body. I continued to leaf through my Bible and came to Hebrews 13:3, a verse I had never read before: 'Remember them that are in bonds [prison], as bound with them; and them which suffer adversity, as being yourselves also in the body' (AV).

I began to pray again. 'Lord, are you allowing me to experience what it's like to be in prison so that I understand? I know I'm here because I did something stupid, but there are many in countries like Russia and China who are in prison just because of their faith.'

I began to try and imagine what it must be like to be incarcerated in the Gulag for twenty years or in a Cuban prison on Castro's Caribbean island. The prospect was unthinkable, yet a living nightmare for hundreds, maybe thousands, of my brothers and sisters around this cruel world of ours.

As I gasped for air in that dank cell I could hear the others quietly chanting Koranic verses to a backdrop of buzzing mosquitoes. I was finally able to sink into a fitful sleep and awoke some hours later, parched and with a terrible headache. I felt feverish and my face had swelled to terrible proportions.

Finally, the cell door was unlocked and a guard shouted at me, 'Hey, white man, you will come next door and speak with the chief immigration officer. But leave your shoes off. We don't want you to try and escape.' His eyes had become ugly slits and I heard a metallic click from his rifle.

The official was equally unsympathetic.

'You can protest all you like, Mr Wooding, but you are still going to be kicked out of our country,' he said with an indifference that chilled me. 'You have arrived without a visa and you cannot enter Nigeria.' His voice dripped with contempt.

I felt tears of frustration welling up in my eyes.

'Can I say something, please.'

He yawned, stretched and nodded as he eased his well-polished boots up onto his well-littered desk.

'I came here with nothing but goodwill for the country of my birth. Now you make me feel ashamed to have those feelings. You are doing all you can to make me hate Nigeria. But that is not going to happen. Jesus told me to love everybody and I'm going to love you people.'

I tried to continue, but he cut in, his eyes bulging from behind his steel-rimmed glasses. 'Okay, enough of the speech,' he said abrasively. 'We are arranging for you to take a flight to London this morning. You can have breakfast here at the airport, but you'll have to pay for it.'

With my shoes returned to me, I was frog-marched at gun-point to the restaurant where I was able to order bacon and eggs. They have never tasted so good! My guard watched my every move with an expression that was both amused and contemptuous.

Back in the cell, I said goodbye to my new-found African friends, and not long afterwards I was told that it was time to leave. I was roughly bundled aboard the plane, and was not allowed to have my passport back until we were in the air.

Norma was shocked when I appeared at our front door and told her what had happened to me. Her voice was soft as she said, 'Don't think it was all a waste of time, Dan. I know the Lord allowed you to experience the prison cell to know what it's like to be locked up. Maybe one day he's going to have you write about people who are imprisoned.'

She paused for a moment, and then added, 'I know it wasn't pleasant for you. But I also know that God doesn't allow anything to happen to us without a reason. One day that reason will become completely clear to you.'

18

Twenty-Six Lead Soldiers

Personal advancement is worth very little if in achieving it one loses one's own sense of peace.

EDWARD EDDY

After four years of stringing, I was offered a job on the *Sunday People's* reporting team. And it wasn't long before I was in the middle of the fray with the other news hounds of Fleet Street in chasing after the big exclusives. This kind of journalism had become very controversial and I quickly learned that money talks. Among the stories I wrote up was Diana Dors' 'love affair' with Elvis Presley; the life of Melody Bugner with her boxing champ husband; and the heart-attack story of Eric Morecambe, the comic from the Morecambe and Wise duo; plus a host of stories with personalities like 'Carry On' actress, Barbara Windsor and comedian, Larry Grayson.

I worked in this frenetic atmosphere for three years.

It was while I was interviewing Eric Morecambe about his illness that my frustrations with my life in Fleet Street began to come to the surface. After listening to his story at his home, I told him that I was having real problems as a Christian coping with some of the ethical problems that

154

faced me.

'Eric, I don't know if my conscience will allow me to stay in Fleet Street much longer,' I told him. 'I think I'm going to have to get out.'

The comedian looked at me very seriously. 'Dan, you are very fortunate to be able to afford a conscience. Most people in this world can't afford to have one!'

I was shocked by what he said. Morecambe was saying that most people just have to survive—whatever it takes. Was that the way Christians should live? Should we just join the rat-race or should we opt out? What was the answer?

Besides the struggles I was having with my conscience, Norma was also concerned with my drinking habits, which usually took place in the smoke-filled Stab in the Back. I justified my large intake of German lager by telling myself that I was just doing the same as my fellow scribes. Besides the booze helped to blunt the pain I felt in dealing with so much human anguish. Because of the type of paper I worked on, we attracted the bizarre, the strange and the tragic. It seemed as if I spent most of my time grubbing around the dustbins of British life. Instead of writing anything worth while, I felt I was just helping to present a freak show of stories for an audience that craved sensation, not beauty.

One reporter in the Stab pulled me up with a jolt one day when he asked me, 'Are you still a Christian, Dan? I see you are becoming as ruthless as us. You go after a story just like we do and use all your guile to get people to "tell all".'

Was I really no different from the others in Fleet Street? Was I actually conning people to talk to me or was that just professionalism?

I had to admit that I enjoyed the chase. I found it a great challenge to be given a story that seemed impossible to get and, against all the odds, filing it hours later. I enjoyed mixing with people like Paul McCartney and

Ringo Starr, the Monty Python team and Burt Lancaster, though I still had many reservations about the underworld characters I had become involved with.

I also harboured a whole series of grudges against people whom I believed had wronged me over the years. One of the worst was when I was nearly sent to jail for contempt for not revealing the source of a story involving a dispute between two Christians. On another occasion, a group of Christians had threatened to sue me over something I had written in a book. My anger had begun to eat away at me like a cancer.

One night Norma talked over the situation with me. She got out her Bible and opened it at 1 Corinthians 6:1-2:

> When one of you has a grievance against a brother, does he dare go to law before the unrighteous instead of the saints? Do you not know that the saints will judge the world? And if the world is to be judged by you, are you incompetent to try trivial cases?

As we discussed the situation, I brought out my bad feelings towards an internationally known singer who had agreed to let me 'ghost' his life story for a book.

'Do you remember that I gave up a considerable amount of time writing the first draft of the manuscript?' I recalled for Norma.

'Suddenly, out of the blue, came a letter from him saying he didn't want the book published after all. No offer of payment for my work, no real explanation. I have to admit that I've felt angry about this situation for a long time now. I've always found that the secular newspapers I've worked for pay up if they ask me to do work. Yet this man wanted me to do the book with him, then dropped it—and me.'

As we spoke, I remembered telling this story to David Aikman, a Christian journalist on *Time* magazine in New York and he said, 'Dan, you have every right to feel hard done by. He has probably treated you very badly. But I want to point out a Scripture to you.'

He showed me Matthew 5:22-24. 'Read it out loud,' he
suggested. 'Maybe God will show you what you should do
towards this man.'

So I opened his Bible and began to read:

> . . . I say to you that every one who is angry with his brother
> shall be liable to judgment . . . So if you are offering your
> gift at the altar, and there remember that your brother has
> something against you, leave your gift there before the altar
> and go; first be reconciled to your brother, and then come and
> offer your gift.

I related the story to Norma. 'You know,' I said sadly,
'I've never taken his advice. Maybe I should apologize to
him for my feelings against him right now.'

I quickly typed out a letter to him and sent it care of his
British record company.

A few days later I received a phone call from an executive of the company.

'I was in the room when he opened your letter,' he told
me. 'He began to cry when he read what you'd written.
He really appreciated your doing what you did.'

The more I pondered it, the more I realized that there
was a lot of poison in my system, and much of it was
directed towards Christians whom I felt had wronged me.

One of those worked for Billy Graham's British office
and I had given him a rough time while working on the
Sunday People. I had even threatened to write a most
unflattering story about him about a petty dispute we had
become embroiled in.

'Dan, the scriptural thing is to apologize to him,' Norma
told me. 'I know it's a painful thing for you to do, but you
must.'

So with great trepidation I phoned him and told him
how sorry I was for my attitude. I later discovered how
distressed he had become over my attitude towards him.

'Thank you, brother,' he told me down the line, his

voice cracking with emotion. 'My big wish is that we can now become friends.'

Although God was dealing with me, I was feeling more and more that my time in Fleet Street was coming to an end. I had served my apprenticeship and I felt that I should be involved in another kind of writing that was not so trivial.

I shared this one day with a close friend.

'Dan, first of all, I know from bitter experience how ruthless and cruel some Christians can be,' he told me. 'All those things you have shared with me I know are true, because I've experienced many of them myself. But I want to tell you something. The most important thing in the world for you at this moment is not who is right and wrong, but your personal relationship with Jesus Christ. Unless you get that right, you will always be full of bitterness and anger. God will judge those who do wrong in his own time, but he will also judge you. Are you ready for that?'

Those words were like a knife to my heart. In my confusion over the lives of those I thought I should look up to, I was forgetting my own shortcomings.

He pointed out Matthew 7:4 to me:

> Or how can you say to your brother, 'Let me take the speck out of your eye,' when there is the log in your own eye? You hypocrite, first take the log out of your own eye, and then you will see clearly to take the speck out of your brother's eye.

That night I got down on my knees before God and asked for forgiveness for straying so far from my original calling as a journalist. I also had to get right with Norma. I realized I had become so involved in my work and the excitement of it, that I had almost completely cut her out of my life.

'Darling, it happened so easily,' I said. 'I got so far along the so-called success trail that I became completely selfish. I brought my work home with me. You and the boys always took second place.'

She held me close and laid her hands on my head.

'Lord,' she prayed, 'please forgive us both for what has happened over the past few years. Help us be one again and begin to serve you as we have been called to.'

Both of us were crying with happiness that we were really back with each other again.

Next day, Ray Barnett called me at the office.

'Dan, I've got another proposition for you,' he said.

'Oh, yes?' I chuckled. 'Last time you did that I nearly got into serious trouble in Russia. So what is it this time?'

'Oh, it's something that may cost you your life . . . .'

When we met for lunch, he told me that he was recently in Uganda. 'While I was there I discovered that Idi Amin has been conducting a real holocaust against the believers. Hundreds of thousands have been murdered by him and his henchmen.

'I hear that much of the finance for the killing is coming from Libya and Saudi Arabia. They want Amin to set up an Islamic state and don't care to what lengths he goes to do it.'

His face became serious.

'Dan, I want to ask you if you would be prepared to give up your job in Fleet Street if Idi Amin falls. Would you go to Uganda with me and get the inside story of what really happened to the church during the last few years? It could be dangerous; it will certainly mean a drop in your standard of living. But what a service you would be doing to the worldwide church of Jesus Christ. And once you've got the story, there are thousands of others around the world you could help. You could become a voice for the suffering church.'

He then told me about a statement attributed to Karl Marx: 'Give me twenty-six lead soldiers and I'll conquer the world.'

'Dan, he meant the alphabet on a typewriter. Marx knew how powerful words can be and you can see how successful his crusade for world domination has been. Are you prepared to use your 'twenty-six lead soldiers' for God?'

It was a question I had soon to answer!

19

Uganda Holocaust

Evil can never be undone, but only purged and redeemed.

DOROTHY SAYERS

It was May 1979, just weeks after Idi Amin had been routed by the Tanzanian Army and had fled to Libya to be sheltered by his friend, Muammar Khadaffy. Ray Barnett and I were heading towards Entebbe Airport to gather the story of the Uganda holocaust. We had managed to secure a book deal for the inside story of what had happened to the Church.

'Well, Dan,' said Ray, 'you've gone and done it.'

I smiled wryly. 'Yes, I have. You know, on the last day at the paper they had a reception and all the staff sang "All things bright and beautiful" for me. I think they must have made history. I don't think a hymn's ever been sung in the *Sunday People* newsroom before.

'I'm glad I'm out, but it was quite a wrench. It was as if I had a ladder up to a building which was my career. I had crawled and scratched my way to the top and when I got there I discovered I had the ladder against the wrong building all the time . . . .'

Just then we touched down at battle-scarred Entebbe.

The passengers, mainly Ugandan refugees returning home, clapped joyously as the hostess said 'Welcome home!'

In Nairobi, we approached World Vision International and they agreed to allow Ray and me to join one of their relief reconnoitres, and to travel with them in a Volkswagen Kombi that would take us on the long, hair-raising journey into the very heart of the Uganda holocaust. Joining Ray and me on that trip was Dan Brewster, an American who was relief and development associate at the World Vision office in Africa.

Now at Entebbe, we clambered down the steps of the plane to be greeted by a hot, stuffy billow of air, and I noticed a huge presence of Tanzanian troops. About three hundred yards from our plane, the notorious 'Whisky Run' jet stood motionless and riddled with bullets. This Boeing 707, bearing the black, red, and yellow insignia of Uganda Airlines, used to make a weekly fourteen-hour flight to Stanstead Airport in England, where Amin's men would load it up with booze (even though they were Muslims) and other 'goodies' for the killer squads. The Ugandans paid for this with cash from the sale of coffee. Often there was as much as forty tons of goods in the airplane's hold. Whisky was always a priority. It was Amin's way of buying their loyalty.

As we walked into the devastated terminal, it was amusing to see a table with a single immigration official, parked in the middle of the twisted mess. I presented my passport and before he even looked at it, he fixed me with a baleful stare and asked in an eerie, controlled voice, 'Do you have any Kenyan newspapers? It gets so boring here with only two flights a day.' (One was from Kenya, the other Zaire.)

I lamely handed him a Nairobi newspaper, so he stamped my passport. Obviously documentation didn't mean too much, as long as I had something for him to read.

When the three of us got through customs, we were met by Geoffrey Latim, a former Olympic athlete who had fled the country during Amin's reign. He was to be our guide. Latim led us to a Christian customs officer who, while being watched by a poker-faced Tanzanian soldier armed with a rifle, made a token check of our bags.

'There's no phone link with Kampala and little or no petrol,' explained Latim. 'So we might be in for a long wait until a driver arrives for us. He dropped me off and said he would be back later.'

Latim was right. During that time, the Christian customs official, who turned out to be from the Acholi tribe, joined us for a chat. He shared with us how God had saved his life. 'I was going to be killed on April 7, 1979,' he said. 'But on the sixth, Entebbe was freed by the Tanzanians and my life was spared.' The man revealed that his name was on a death list found when the State Research Bureau headquarters at Nakasero, Kampala, was liberated by the Tanzanians. He looked sad as he told of the heartbreak of his job during Amin's rule. 'I saw many people passing through customs and I knew there was no way they would reach the aircraft,' he said tragically. 'They would be intercepted by the State Research men and never be heard of again. These terrible killers were all over the airport. Most of them were illiterate and had got their jobs because they were of the same tribe as Amin.'

Eventually the Kombi arrived and we began the thirty-mile journey to the capital. We were stopped at several road blocks set up by the Tanzanians, and Latim patiently explained to the positively wild-looking soldiers—most of whom were carrying a rifle in one hand, a huge looted 'ghetto-blaster' playing loud, thumping disco music in the other—why we were in Uganda. Burned-out military hardware, including tanks, littered the sides of the main highway to Kampala.

Soon we were at the Namirembe Guest House, run by the Church of Uganda, but originally set up by the Church

Missionary Society. It was getting dark as the van bumped its way into the grounds, which are just below the cathedral.

'You are all most welcome,' said the ever-smiling manager, Naomi Gonahasa. We soon realized the incredible difficulties under which she and her staff were working. There was no running water and so it had to be brought in jerry cans from the city on the back of a bicycle, at a pound a can.

Each resident was rationed to one bottle of brownish water per day—and that was for everything. They had no gas for cooking, so it was all done on a charcoal fire. What made it even more difficult was that there were no telephones working in the entire city, so we could not alert any of Ray's contacts that we had arrived.

When we unpacked in the fading light, we heard the sounds of machine-gun fire reverberating across the city below us. Then came the sounds of heavy explosions and of screaming and wailing, which continued all through the night.

I now realized that Ray had been deadly serious when he told me that this trip could cost me my life. I got down by my bed and committed my life to the Lord.

'God,' I said against a background of screaming, 'I don't know what is going to happen here, but I want you to have your own way with my life, and that of Ray. We realize the dangers, but they are nothing to what our brothers and sisters here have faced over the past eight years.'

As I stood up, I turned to Ray who was calmly lying on his bed, reading his Bible, and said, 'A fine mess you've got me into again . . . .'

He smiled.

'Where would you rather be—in Fleet Street, or here, serving the suffering church of Uganda?'

My look showed him that I knew I was in the centre of God's will.

During our stay at the guest house, we became firm friends with Naomi and her husband Stephen. As we built up trust with them, they revealed their part in saving the lives of believers on the run from Amin's savage killers.

I learned from them the secret code word which they responded to when someone came to them for sanctuary.

'This was a good hiding place from State Research people,' said Stephen. 'People would turn up here and as long as they knew the code word "Goodyear", we would hide them. Their food was served in their rooms. Naturally we would not let them sign the guest register in case it would be checked.'

Naomi added, 'We were not really frightened, because we believed that God was protecting us.'

This sincere young couple, obvious targets for the State Research, were also active members of an underground church. Often believers from the Deliverance Church, one of the twenty-seven groups banned by Amin after receiving orders from Allah in dreams, would have meetings in the lounge of the guest house.

Next morning we had our first experience of the terrible ferocity of Amin's battle against the church during his reign of terror. We went to a church in Makerere, run by the Gospel Mission to Uganda. As we examined the bullet holes that had riddled the ceiling and the walls, I asked a member what had happened.

He told me that on April 12, 1978, Amin's wild-eyed soldiers had invaded the church and begun firing indiscriminately at the 600-strong congregation. Assistant pastor, Jotham Mutebi, was on the platform and he sank to his knees in prayer.

Amid the mayhem, hundreds more quickly dropped to their knees between the pews. With upraised arms they began to praise the Lord. The sturdy red brick church was filled with a cacophony of incredible sound—a combination of prayer, praise and bullets.

Joseph Nyakairu, a member of the church orchestra,

raised his trumpet to his lips and blew it as loudly as he could. The Amin soldiers thought the Christians were about to counter-attack and fled the sanctuary.

In the ensuing confusion, nearly 400 people managed to slip away from the church. But at least 200 remained on their knees and continued to worship the Lord when the soldiers returned and continued spraying bullets everywhere. They took hold of Joseph's trumpet and threw it to the ground, spraying bullets at it. Then they 'executed' the organ. The congregation knew that death could be imminent and that they were under arrest!

They were taken to the State Research Bureau headquarters at Nakasero, and there they were mocked and told that as soon as General Mustafa Adrisi, Idi Amin's second-in-commmand, signed the execution order, they would all be burned alive.

The 200 sat in silent prayer and even as they prayed General Adrisi was involved in a terrible car crash in which both his legs were badly fractured.

'He ended up a cripple in a wheelchair and finally Amin turned against him,' said one believer.

When the signed order from Adrisi did not appear, the guards led the prisoners to the cells. They were kept behind bars for some months. Many of them were badly tortured, but miraculously none of them died.

As we left these incredible people, I turned to Ray and said, 'I've never met believers of this calibre in my country. They certainly have much to teach us about faith and courage.'

We bumped along for hours on end, having to stop regularly at road blocks.

In Latim's hometown of Gulu, we learned the astonishing story of the burial of Archbishop Janani Luwum, who had been brutally shot in the mouth by Idi Amin himself.

Mildred Brown, an English woman who was working in the region translating the Scriptures into Acholi for the Bible Society, began to explain how Janani's body had been taken to his home village of Mucwini, near the Sudan border, for burial.

His mother, at her home, told the soldiers, 'My son is a Christian. He cannot be buried here, he must be buried in the graveyard of the local church.'

So the soldiers took the coffin to the picturesque tiny hilltop church for a hurried burial.

As we drank our tea, Miss Brown told us, 'The soldiers had begun to dig the grave, but hadn't been able to complete the job before dark because the earth was too hard. They left the coffin in the church overnight, so they could finish the grave the next day.'

Thus the hardness of the ground gave the group of believers at Mucwini the chance to gaze for the last time on their martyred archbishop. By the flickering gleam of a hurricane lamp, they saw the body of a purple-clad man. They noted there were two gun wounds, one in his neck, where the bullet had apparently gone into his mouth and out again, the other in his groin. Janani's purple robe was stained with blood, his arms were badly skinned, his rings had been stolen, and he was shoeless.

They were all gazing quietly, reverently, at the body of a martyr, a man who was killed for daring to stand up to the black Hitler of Africa.

Even as the people gave thanks for their beloved archbishop, just one of some 500,000 victims under Amin, the government-controlled newspaper, *Voice of Uganda,* published a call for President Amin to be made emperor and then proclaimed Son of God.

Our trip into the heart of Amin's holocaust even took us into Karamoja, where naked men and boys would run across the track brandishing spears.

Famine was rife in that region. Our final memory of Karamoja was the old lady who was too weak to move, sitting silently in the village of Kotido. The woman, who appeared to be near death, squatted by her open hut to keep out of the sun's rays. She said through an interpreter that she had eaten only wild greens for two months. She displayed large folds of loose skin around her rib cage.

Famine, more than Idi Amin, had taken its toll in Karamoja.

Back in Kampala, we were able to meet up with 'God's Double Agent in the President's Office'. Ben Oluka, who was senior assistant secretary in the Department of Religious Affairs in Amin's office, had used his influence to bring about the saving of many Christian lives throughout Uganda.

But what Amin did not realize was that Ben Oluka was not only doing what he could to assist suffering believers, but was also pastoring an underground church in his home. It was a small group from the Deliverance Church, an indigenous Ugandan evangelical fellowship.

'At that time, I was working in the office that had to enforce the president's ban (against the twenty-seven denominations), and secretly I was running an underground church myself,' he said. 'When the ban was announced, much of the church immediately went underground, and house meetings sprang up throughout the country. There is a higher power, and when government restricts freedom of worship, God's supremacy has to take over. *I was personally ready for martyrdom.*'

And that was the feeling of millions of Ugandan believers, regardless of Amin's persecution. They were willing to die for Christ.

I returned from Uganda a different person. The courage of the Ugandan Christians will live with me for ever.

'After working on a story like this, how can I ever return to Fleet Street?' I shared with Norma back home.

'You know, as I was travelling around with Ray interviewing and photographing these incredible people, I was reminded of a story I wrote all those years ago at *The Christian*.'

Norma looked at me quizzically.

'Do you remember the story of Bill Howe, that spastic

patient who was taught to communicate by those nurses at the hospital. They taught him to "speak" through his toe. If it hadn't been for them he would never have had a voice. I wonder if God is calling me to be a "voice" for the Christians suffering all over the world for Christ.'

Norma's face creased into a huge smile. She became quiet and contemplative.

'Dan, if that is what the Lord is telling you to do, I'm thrilled. But I wonder if the excitement and lure of Fleet Street will be too much for you to resist.'

20

The Land where Fidel Is God

Power is the ultimate aphrodisiac.

HENRY KISSINGER

It was as if my father had been transported to Havana.
The little old man who rushed towards me as I entered the
Havana church was the spitting image of Dad.

'You're the one,' he said rapidly. 'I knew you would
come and pray for me!'

My father's grey-haired double, his eyes moist with
tears, continued, 'Yes, I had a dream that some visitors
would come from abroad and that one of them—you—
would pray for me so that I would receive a special blessing. It was your face I saw in the dream.'

I put my arm around his frail shoulders and began praying for him. As I did, I spared a thought for my father who
was some 4,000 miles away. He was now retired and living
outside of Liverpool with my mother. Now here I was in
Cuba, at the beginning of a new chapter in my life.

Suddenly the old man was sobbing deeply. Several
other believers joined with our team of Open Doors couriers for a time of prayer. Soon another Cuban began
weeping and for thirty minutes the two cried like babies.

170

At the end of this moving prayer time, the elderly man wiped his tears and then thrust his arms around me and hugged me tight. I don't usually make people cry, so I was quite taken aback by what had just happened.

'Why are you so unhappy?' I asked him as he continued to hold me tight.

'I'm not unhappy,' he said as he loosened his grip. 'These are tears of joy. You are the first believer from England to come here in the past twenty years to encourage us. You don't know what it means to us to realize that we are not forgotten!'

This surprise meeting took place shortly after I had completed my work on *God's Smuggler to China*. Brother Andrew had asked me to go to Cuba to learn about the situation of the church there after years of rule by Fidel Castro, and also to do research for the book *Prophets of Revolution*.

I had been diverted back into Fleet Street in 1980 after completing *Uganda Holocaust*. I was running low on funds to feed my family, and so had taken a job with another Fleet Street paper. But it was not to be. I had now got a taste of what it was like to serve the suffering church and was praying that somehow a new opportunity would open up.

I arrived home one Friday night and told Norma my heart was no longer in my work. 'I really believed the Lord had called me to be a "voice" for the suffering church, yet I gave up at the first hurdle,' I said in disgust. 'What can I do? I feel trapped.'

Norma squeezed my hand and said, 'Well, one thing you can do, Dan, is to call Ed Neteland in California. He phoned you earlier this afternoon. Do you remember, he's the guy you met there who is the Executive Vice President of Open Doors with Brother Andrew.'

'What does he want?' I asked, wondering if it was to do with previous conversations about my desire to serve persecuted Christians as a writer.

I called Ed and he dispensed with the usual niceties and launched straight into the reason for his call.

'Dan,' he said in his soft American accent, 'I believe God wants you to write a book with a man called Brother David, who has been heading up our work into China for many years. I've booked a ticket in faith for you to fly to Manila on Sunday morning. What do you say?'

What could I say but, 'I'll make the flight.'

The initial three weeks with Brother David, a former American Marine and football player, was just the sign that I needed from God that this was to be my life from now on. Here was a man obedient to God who had been used to get large quantities of Bibles into China, including one million on June 18, 1981, during what was called Project Pearl.

I came back to England all fired up and handed in my notice at the newspaper. Norma was full of encouragement as I told her of my decision to leave Fleet Street for good.

She grabbed her Bible, opened it at Romans 8:28, and read, 'We know that in everything God works for good with those who love him, who are called according to his purpose.'

She closed the pages and said, 'Dan, the Apostle Paul says that "in everything God works for good . . . ." That includes your time in Fleet Street.

'Don't you see? You couldn't understand what a story is, work under great pressure, and interview people in the way you do if you hadn't had that experience.

'I believe Fleet Street was allowed by God to equip you for a much more important ministry—to tell the world about believers who are suffering for Jesus. You can tell millions about what they are going through and what lessons we can learn from them.'

It wasn't long before I was back in Manila for another five weeks of work with Australian Sara Bruce to complete the first draft of *God's Smuggler to China*. It was shortly after this that Brother Andrew asked me to go to Cuba.

I had been pleased when he had told me, 'You don't need to take in Bibles on this particular trip. For if you get caught, it could spoil your research.'

But I hadn't reckoned on Peter. I had stopped en route at a Miami hotel where I met the other members of the team to be led by Mexican-born Peter Gonzales. He marched into my room laden down with an armful of Bibles, Christian books, music cassettes and car tools.

'Here you are, Dan. Can you tuck these away in your suitcase?' he asked. He had a similar bundle for my room mate, Terry.

'But,' I protested, 'I thought I was only coming along to report on the trip—not to carry "goods".'

He faced me with an expression that said, 'If you won't carry them, that means the rest of us will have even more to put in our already full bags.'

I felt quite ashamed. Here was a courageous group of couriers who were prepared to trust the Lord to get those goods through Cuban customs and I just wanted to be an onlooker. But, I reasoned, isn't that what a journalist is supposed to be? We stood on the sidelines, but rarely got involved. We were really a bunch of voyeurs!

Then he delivered the knock-out punch. 'Don't you want to see God do a miracle?' What could I say? 'Okay, you win,' I said holding up my hands. 'I surrender!'

The fact that I was to be a Bible courier put a new perspective on the trip for me. Instead of just being an outsider reporting on the suffering church, I was now to be part of a team ministering to them. That meant I would have to be completely dependent on the Lord for getting the cargo through customs and making contact with the believers inside. What a frightening thought that was.

The pre-flight prayer meeting in Peter's room made all of us agonize before the Lord. We knew that since Castro had overthrown the dictator Fulgencio Batista more than twenty-one years earlier, Christian believers had been under constant pressure from the Communist government.

'Lord,' prayed Peter, who had been to Cuba before, 'we are not relying on our cleverness to get these much-needed items through the Cuban customs, but on your greatness. We ask you to blind the eyes of the officials.'

Peter's usually good-humoured face was still as he instructed us not to lie to customs. But, naturally, he also told us not to say we were taking in Christian books and Bibles unless asked directly.

'We are to obey God rather than men and he has commanded us to go and strengthen that which remains,' he continued. 'That is why we are going into Cuba.'

Then he went a step further and asked me not to even try to hide the Bibles in my clothing, but to put them on top of them. 'Then you will see God do a real miracle,' he said.

'But that's crazy,' I responded desperately. 'They'll obviously see them if they open my suitcase.'

'Just trust the Lord,' was his parting comment.

I don't think I have ever prayed as much as I did on that bumpy ninety-minute flight over the Caribbean.

Jose was the first to pick up his luggage, and he almost dashed towards the customs officer, a middle-aged woman. It was obvious that he wanted to get the ordeal over as soon as possible. The woman began a slow, deliberate, twenty-minute, unsmiling search of his bags. My heart was pounding as I watched in silence.

I caught my breath as the woman discovered some of the Spanish hymnbooks he had put in on his own. There was a look of triumph on her face as she confiscated them. Then she found the car tools for the pastors and some ballpoint pens.

'Who are these for?' she barked. Jose shrugged his shoulders. 'Could be anyone,' he said in a non-committal way.

The stony-faced official, after staring it out with him, consulted her watch, and to our great relief, waved Jose through and went off duty.

Her place was taken by a black man who hardly spoke any English. He was politeness itself, as if trying to make up for the rudeness of his colleague.

'What do you declare?' he asked me in pidgin English. I pointed to my watch, camera, and tape recorder which I had already laid out on the counter. He studied my declaration which also included a radio. To my horror, I then realized that the radio was in the suitcase along with the Bibles, books and tapes.

'Open up your case.' he said fixing an unflinching gaze on me as a sick, sinking feeling rose in my stomach.

That was the order I had been dreading.

'Okay, Lord,' I whispered, 'I'm in your hands.'

I took a deep breath and did what he asked. I gingerly opened the zip, and then he took over. There were the black Bibles for all to see. I had hoped they would disappear, but they hadn't. I stood transfixed as he pushed them out of the way and felt around inside the clothing until he found the radio.

'Okay, sir, you may go . . .' he said gently. Surely he had seen the books. Or had he? Had God actually blinded his eyes to them?

I gratefully closed the suitcase and headed, as if walking on air, for the exit. As I ran towards the bus that was to take us to Havana, a tropical downpour greeted me, but it was like a deluge of God's tears of joy that more of his family would receive his word.

I took my seat next to Jose, and we both silently thanked the Lord that we were safely through. Then we began interceding for the others who were still going through the ordeal.

Soon, the rest of the team safely joined us on the bus, and we again thanked the Lord for allowing us to bring through customs everything we had packed in Miami, except for Jose's hymnbooks.

We were a joyous group as we ate that night in our hotel located several miles outside of Havana.

Our first contact was to be with a pastor in the capital. Peter observed that almost everyone in Havana seemed to be carrying shoulder bags, so we decided to pack a few items in a bag to be carried by Terry, and to take a public bus into the city centre. It was fascinating to see what had become of this once-wild city. It was like a ghost town.

After wandering around the city centre unsuccessfully trying to make eye contact with the people, we came into a large square and noticed hundreds of school children milling around the school. Most of them wore red bandannas around their necks.

'They are Young Pioneers,' explained Peter. 'And are members of Cuba's Communist youth movement.'

It was depressing to see so many youngsters already indoctrinated in atheism. Fidel obviously knew that if he could brainwash Cuba's children from an early age, he would possibly have them for life.

I stopped some of the pioneers and asked if I could photograph them. They were delighted and took turns in posing. As I waved good-bye and began walking away, a delightful girl aged about twelve came over, took off her red Communist badge and handed it to me.

'Take it, please,' she said. 'It will remind you of our great revolution.'

We continued walking and soon we were completely lost. We frequently came across a house or building with a sign outside which read: 'Committee for the Defence of the Revolution.' Peter explained, 'They are what Fidel calls the "ears and eyes of the revolution". The members of these committees watch everyone on their block and especially look out for what they consider "counter-revolutionary activities". It is a very effective way of controlling the people.'

Eventually we came across the church we were looking

for. From the outside it was a shabby-looking sanctuary, but we soon discovered it housed some wonderful believers. Peter told us to stay out of sight while he made the first approach.

'Remember, if we get into trouble, we will probably only be told to leave the country. But one mistake could mean imprisonment for the people here,' he warned.

Peter crossed the road and darted inside as we tried to make ourselves inconspicuous. After several minutes, he reappeared and signalled to us to come across. The church was located on a busy road, and we were naturally concerned that people would see us going inside and report us to the local Committee for the Defence of the Revolution (CDR). But then, at the very moment we were crossing the road, a huge lorry pulled up in front of the church entrance and blocked the view for anyone watching us.

Inside, the pastor guardedly shook hands with us and signalled us to follow him to his office. Peter had already explained to him who we were.

The pastor was soon joined in the office by his wife, a tall woman with dark eyes and, as the trust was built up, he volunteered to tell us his story.

'Some ten years ago,' he began, 'I was working as an engineer. I wanted to leave the country and so applied for an exit visa for myself, my wife and children.

'Once you do that, the government here considers you dead. You have to sign over everything you have to them. That meant I lost my job, my car and my home. I had to work in the fields.

'Then came the day when we were due to leave. We were all very excited, but as we were about to board the plane for Miami, a military official stopped us and said, "You cannot leave." They did not return anything to me. I had no car, furniture or job. It was very hard.'

The pastor told us it was then that he began to realize that God wanted him to remain in the country of his birth, and eventually he became a pastor.

'Would you like to see how I live?' he asked.

We nodded.

With that, he led us to the basement of the church and showed us how he and his wife—the children now lived away from home—had been able to arrange some furniture in the corners of a large underground garage.

'It's very simple, but it's home to us,' the pastor smiled, as he clasped his wife's hand.

He eventually disclosed that although he was a leader of his particular denomination, his salary amounted to the equivalent of just eighteen pounds a week. Yet, despite his poverty, he and his wife regularly took in lodgers and fed them out of their meagre earnings.

'We always have something for them. It never runs out. The Lord provides . . .' said his wife.

'Even if you have money, it can still be difficult,' she whispered. 'For instance, we are allowed only four ounces of meat per person every ten days. The rationing here is very strict. As for clothing, I am allowed to buy my husband a shirt and one pair of trousers per year. I can also get him a pair of shoes in the official shops and markets. There is what we call a parallel market, where prices are sky high, but you can still buy if you can afford it.'

The pastor then revealed that he could have gone to the United States in 1980 along with the 100,000 Cubans who left in the Mariel flotilla of boats.

'Some of my congregation left and they asked me to go with them, but I wouldn't. My place is here with my flock. The Lord has been very good. He has already replaced all the members who left then.'

As we talked, two teenage youths opened the door without knocking and came into the room. We were eventually introduced to them. The pastor explained that they had both been university students, who, after the CDR had discovered they were Christians, were deprived of their places. Both now did menial jobs.

'We are supposed to report to the CDR anyone who

gets baptized,' he continued. 'Of course we do, but we usually put off the baptism until we are really sure that they can withstand all that goes with it.'

Peter then brought out some of the Bibles and books we had with us. The pastor gasped and fondly began examining the books.

Another pastor came into the room. He had recently been released from prison.

'Why were you there?' I asked.

He smiled wryly and cleared his throat. 'They said I was working for the CIA,' he said, almost reflectively. 'They said that of all of us who belong to denominations that have American connections.'

Shortly after our discussions began, Peter produced more Bibles and books and handed them to him. The man was taken aback. He didn't say thank you but just clasped them with both hands.

'To me this is the most precious thing in the world,' he whispered. 'More precious than gold.'

When we returned to the hotel, we passed safely through the security that surrounds all Cuban hotels. We were alarmed, however, to see a man embrace Peter in front of other guests. Peter introduced us to him. He turned out to be a pastor who had travelled nearly 300 miles to see us. Peter had decided to give him a suitcase of items including clothes for his family and congregation. (He was the leader of another evangelical denomination.) His early arrival—he shouldn't have come until the following day—concerned us.

'Look, brother, you can stay in my room,' said Jose. 'I'd look upon it as a privilege if you would.'

The pastor was smuggled up to Jose's room and there they began a guarded conversation. The talked in whispers just in case the room was bugged. Jose eventually presented him with his small transistor radio.

Later Jose told us what happened:

'He just lay back on his bed with the little radio clasped

to his ear, a big smile on his face. He told me he would now be able to feed his spirit with Christian radio programmes that come in from other countries. He said it would be his lifeline to the outside world.'

The next morning we were confronted with a problem. Somehow we had to get the large suitcase bulging with books and clothes out past the guard and then load it into a car coming to collect us. We picked up bags containing our personal belongings, and Peter took the large case and walked out to the front of the hotel.

Horror of horrors, there was no car waiting for us. We all stood there with the offending suitcase for ten minutes, then twenty then thirty. The hotel guard was becoming suspicious and came over to inspect the case. At that moment I got out my camera to try and distract him. I took his picture. I indicated I wanted to take more. He straightened up and gave me a large grin. Then Jose engaged him in conversation. Between us we kept the guard talking until the 'driver' arrived in his antique car.

Then another problem arose. Our contact was apparently not to be trusted. 'He could be a government informer,' said the pastor anxiously. 'Be careful what you tell him. He could be dangerous.'

The pastor who had come to collect us, we later discovered, had himself once been accused and imprisoned and it was feared that, under threats, he had become an informer. The incident brought home to us what it is like to live as a believer under a Communist system.

'We must not judge him because we have never had to face what he has,' said Peter later.

Discussions at that time revealed there were an estimated fifty believers imprisoned for their faith—that was out of an estimated 100,000 born-again Christians in the whole country.

'The authorities tolerate us only because they prefer to know who we are, rather than have an underground church which they would fear very much,' said one

Christian leader.

I asked if Bibles were banned in Cuba. 'No, they are not banned, but the ones we have are mostly very old,' said one pastor, who showed us his crumbling Bible.

'We don't have new ones for converts. That is a real need, because there are so many.'

But hadn't the Cuban Council of Churches recently arranged for Bible distribution on the island?

'Yes, they were allowed by the government to distribute 10,000 throughout Cuba,' said one pastor. 'That meant that for my congregation of eighty, I received only fifteen.'

Another pastor said he had received ninety Bibles for his congregation of 300.

'We still desperately need brothers like yourselves to bring Bibles and Christian books when they visit our country,' he said. 'It is the main way we can feed our sheep.'

During one meeting with pastors, they began to ask about the church in the rest of the world. 'How are the brethren in China? Russia? America? England? We pray for them all the time.'

At the end of the gathering, one of them said he would like to sing for us. There, unaccompanied, his face shining, he started singing in Spanish. The words began, 'Over the sunset mountain, someday I'll softly go into the arms of Jesus. He, who has loved me so . . . .' He said that when they finally get to be with Jesus, there will be no more tears, no more persecution. It was a beautiful ending to the get-together and really expressed their hope in Jesus.

Back at the hotel, we were brought down to earth when Jose recounted the story of a conversation he had had earlier with a hard-line Cuban Communist. He said he had told the man that he had been troubled because there seemed to be an anti-God feeling in the country.

'Well, that is true,' said the Cuban. 'The reason for it is

that there is no God. Well, not in the sense that you mean it. Fidel is our God. What really lasts are the words of Lenin and Fidel.'

'But,' interrupted Jose, 'what about eternity, what about the beyond?'

'Oh,' retorted the man, 'that is an imperialistic concept. Just pie in the sky. Our eternity is living now.'

Jose continued to try to gently share with the man his faith. When he mentioned the name of Jesus Christ, the man said excitedly, 'Jesus Christ. He was a true revolutionary!'

At the end of our stay, Peter took us for a walk and shared some of his convictions with us.

'I think first and foremost we should pray for Fidel and his government here, that they may come to know Christ and experience the true revolution of love,' he said.

'We should do all we can to encourage our Cuban brothers and sisters through prayer, also through letters, although we should be most careful what we write.

'Obviously, believers coming in to see them is vitally important. It is such a blessing for Cuban Christians to know there are people who care for them and are concerned for their welfare. It is a great stimulus to them to see believers from outside. You know, with so much oppression around them, they can lose hope. If they do, it will be our fault in the West. We must never forget them.

'I am sure the regime wants all the believers to leave and go to the United States. They have already off-loaded the criminals and the lunatics in the Mariel flotilla. Now to have all the Christians leave would suit their purposes very well.'

Peter warned that Fidel Castro's aspirations are not just for Cuba, but for the rest of Latin America. 'It's a case of *have revolution will travel . . . .*'

Throughout the trip many of us talked discreetly to several of the hotel guests about our faith. On the day we left, Peter was able to give 'farewell gifts' to some of the staff at the hotel, who had politely refused all tips. The gifts were New Testaments.

The final 'gift' went to a sad-faced old man who carried our cases to the bus.

'Please take this as a gift from me,' Peter said as he passed the New Testament to the man. 'It is something that means everything to me.'

We had fully expected him to hand it back, but he didn't. 'I know what this is,' he said, a smile breaking out on his lined face. 'I was a Catholic before the revolution. Then I lost my faith. But now I am going to read this. I know it will be good for me and my family . . . very good.'

I learned so much from these courageous believers and I longed to be with more people of this calibre. My desires were soon to be fulfilled. I hardly had the chance to spend time with Norma and the boys in Walton-on-Thames before I was off again on my travels. This time to the 'land of the smoking gun'—El Salvador.

21

'Have A Nice Day—
But Be Careful!'

The purpose of terror is to terrify.

LENIN

The young boy put down the cases in our San Salvador room and smiled politely.

'Thank you, sir,' he said as I handed him a tip. 'Now you have a nice day.' He paused as if to add emphasis, then added, *'But be careful!'*

His warning continued to ring in my ears. It was June 1981, and I was in a country in which the Roman Catholic Church reported that 22,000 had been killed in seventeen months. A place where civilian and military leaders struggled for control within the current US-backed government with a monstrous overkill of bitterness and acrimony. Where leftist elements were fighting to over-throw the government, and where appeals were being made from both sides—the leftists and the government—for popular support.

Sadly, many of the people whom both professed to help were being slaughtered in the name of The Cause.

I had gone to the hemisphere's smallest mainland nation which packs in around five million people, with Peter

Gonzales, Jose and Manuel, a Nicaraguan pastor now living in Costa Rica. We wanted to meet with believers there and discover at first hand what was going on in the midst of the current blood-letting that made even the terrible events in Northern Ireland seem mild in comparison.

'Lord,' I had prayed earnestly before leaving, 'please help us to encourage the believers in El Salvador, and let them teach us many things.'

When we arrived at the modern San Salvador airport, I immediately noticed how empty the place was.

'Only crazy people like us and journalists on assignment come here these days,' whispered Peter, as we headed towards the one immigration official on duty.

A twenty-year-old pastor met us at the barrier and told us that he hadn't been able to get a taxi driver to take us on the one-hour trip to San Salvador City, and he had had to persuade a minibus driver to transport us on the risky thirty-mile journey.

'Not too many people want to do this trip,' he explained. 'It's so dangerous. Only yesterday, a vehicle carrying newsmen was ambushed on this road by terrorists. Two people died.'

As we drove on, the young pastor shared that he had left his country a year previously because he found that many of the Christian young people, including himself, were being pressurized to join one of the many Marxist movements. He said he wanted nothing to do with the violence.

'While in another Central American country I met with this brother,' he said pointing to Manuel. 'He showed me how to organize cell groups and set about winning the hearts of our youth through a revolution of love—not hate.'

As we conversed, the driver suddenly swerved and headed off the road and onto a hilly track. Rocks had been placed across the road, a typical ploy used in ambushes. Whether this was one or not, the driver still took

swift evasive action. After bumping our way up one side
of the hill and down the other side, we were eventually
back on the main road.

The city had obviously, at one time, been quite beautiful. The modern capital of San Salvador is situated in the
Valle de las Hamacas (Valley of the Hammocks), and is
laid out in the form of a cross.

'It seems as if the whole place is being crucified by the
violence,' I observed to the driver as I noted the bomb
damage everywhere.

He nodded sadly.

After unpacking at the almost-empty hotel, Peter outlined the plan for the rest of the day.

'This afternoon we are going into one of the worst
ghettos in the city . . . .'

I was startled.

'Couldn't we just stay in the hotel room and the people
come to us?' I protested.

Peter, a seasoned traveller in Central America, wasn't
having any of that.

'No,' he said firmly, 'the young pastor has arranged a
house meeting there for the young people. He wants us to
speak to them.'

I thought quickly. It occurred to me that my white skin
could cause problems not only for me, but for my com-
panions. Was this a way out for me?

'Look Peter, I'll stand out like a sore thumb,' I said
lamely. 'Maybe you could go and I'll stay here and
pray . . . .'

I could see from Peter's face that no excuses would be
tolerated. He pointed out that I hadn't travelled all this
way from England to lock myself away in the relative
safety of a hotel room.

Peter found a taxi driver parked nervously outside the
hotel who agreed to take us to the address the pastor had
scribbled down.

'Are you a journalist?' the middle-aged driver asked

Peter, speeding along as if taking part in a Grand Prix.

'No, I'm not,' he said firmly. 'I've come here because I love this country and want to see what is happening to tear it apart.'

The driver's voice came back like a fast serve.

'Well, I don't believe you. Only journalists come here. But whatever, I want to thank you for coming. You are very brave—all of you.'

I didn't feel very courageous, silently praying in the back of the taxi. I was scared to death. I felt as if every eye in San Salvador was boring in on me and people were hissing, 'Gringo. We hate gringos. We kill gringos.'

(This is a term for white North Americans, but often used for Europeans as well.)

After driving around the area for some time, the perspiring driver could not locate the exact address and began to panic.

'It's not safe for me to stay here much longer,' he said, his voice trembling with terror. 'Please get out now and ask someone for directions.'

He mopped his brow in panic.

The three of us had no alternative but to climb out. We began vainly searching for the address we needed. For ten heart-stopping minutes, we walked around the rabbit-warren of alleyways trying not to be conspicuous, but knowing that at any minute one, or all of us, could be killed.

It was my first experience of racialism. Many in El Salvador support the Marxist groups and I was a white man, so therefore represented oppression. It was frightening to be on the wrong end of mindless hatred. Something, I pondered, coloured people had known for years.

When we finally found the young pastor's house, he greeted us warmly and then said, 'Oh, no, the meeting isn't here. It's back there.' He pointed to where we had just come from.

For another twelve minutes—I timed it—we followed

him through the 'warren' until we finally came upon a bungalow. A few young people milled around in the alley and looked in astonishment as they saw me.

Inside, a small group of women and girls were preparing a meal. When they saw my white face, all talking stopped. Obviously, my presence put them all in danger. And they knew it.

'Is this a funeral?' commented the exasperated pastor. 'Look, our friend has come all the way from England,' he said looking at my ashen face. 'Don't look so glum. Jesus is here and he will protect us.'

Trestle tables had been laid out for what was described as 'Open house with food', a unique way for the young pastor and his small group of converts to evangelize to the ghetto.

As I sat quietly watching a trickle of swarthy young men come into the room, Peter leaned over and said quietly, 'Don't be alarmed, but there is a possibility that some of those here are terrorists who have come to cause trouble. There's been a lot of killing in the area recently. Only yesterday there was a battle between the National Guard and the terrorists living in here.'

Peter conversed freely with three young men sitting across from us.

One told him: 'I've just come out of prison. I was accused of being a terrorist. I was tortured for thirteen days. It was terrible. I've just been here a few minutes, and already I can feel the love in this place.'

After a delicious meal served to more than fifty packed into the front room of the house, the young pastor began explaining to the group why they had been invited.

'Look Dan,' said Peter urgently as the preacher continued, 'maybe you shouldn't speak after all. A "gringo" might upset them and cause real trouble.'

I was inclined to agree. But just then I heard Manuel say, 'Now we have a friend from England. I want him to come and say a few words to you.'

I was unable to protest, so with Peter as my translator, I simply explained how as a teenager I had been a rebel and had left my home in Birmingham to live in Canada.

'I was full of hatred for my parents and for the whole world,' I said, my voice trembling with nerves. 'But eventually I realized how terrible hate can be and through a serious illness that came on my father, I swallowed my pride, went back home and accepted Christ into my life.

'With that, all my anger went and was replaced with love. I know that many of you here today have hate in your hearts. But Jesus can take that away and replace it with the revolution of love.'

As I sat down, I noticed the trickle of a tear appear on the tanned cheek of one of the young men near the front.

Peter then preached for twenty minutes. More began to weep as he outlined God's plan of salvation for them.

'Don't throw away your life in mindless violence. Give it to Jesus and let him use you here in El Salvador,' he urged. 'Join the greatest revolutionary in the history of the world—Jesus Christ!'

He then asked the young people to respond to the claims of Christ. More than half of them stood up and indicated that they wished to follow Jesus. It was an emotional moment for all of us.

Some came and threw their arms around us, and several confessed to a violent past. One young man who could hardly walk because of a painful foot injury, asked me to come and personally pray for him. I clasped my arm around him and asked the Lord to heal him.

'Thank you for coming,' he said afterwards. 'Not many people come here to us now.'

After more than an hour of shaking hands with the 'new-born' believers, we managed to flag down a taxi outside to take us back to the hotel.

That evening we went to a coffee shop for our meal. As I was eating my steak, Peter smiled wryly and said, 'Did you realize that just two weeks ago some gunmen walked into this very coffee shop and shot two journalists who were eating here?'

'Peter, don't tell me things like that,' I said as I picked unenthusiastically at my meal.

Next morning, a Christian leader came to see us and took us on a tour of the city. We went from one bombed-out building to the next. It was a depressing experience.

As we came to one spot in the city, he turned and said, 'See that wall there. Well, my wife and four children were put up against it with me a few days ago and we were to be executed by government troops. We had just come out of church and there had been trouble in the area. The soldiers took us out of the car at a road block and accused us of being a Marxist cell group.

'Just as they had the rifles pointed at us I was able to persuade the leader to look in the back of my car. There he found books and Bibles, and finally agreed that we were Christians, and let us go. *God saved our lives!*'

I asked him if there was a shortage of Bibles in El Salvador.

'There is,' he said. 'Not because they are banned, but because there is such a demand for them. As soon as they become available, they're snapped up.'

The man dropped us off at the Evangelistic Centre, headquarters of the Assemblies of God, who have an estimated 75,000 members in the country, or half of the Protestant population.

There we met Manuel Quinones Aquillon, president of CESAD (Salvadoran Evangelical Committee for Relief and Development). He told me that the interdenominational committee had sought to aid the more than 300,000 people who have been temporarily displaced at one time or another by the fighting. He said they provided food, clothing, medicines and spiritual counsel. Its policy was to help anyone who does not bear arms.

Aquillon said, 'Jesus tells us in the Bible that when we help one of these people we are helping him. We are doing this work for his glory.'

Like other evangelical groups in the country, he confirmed that despite the turmoil, something of a revival is taking place in El Salvador.

'One of the biggest lessons the church has learned here is that we must reach the children and young people with the gospel, otherwise they will join the subversive groups and probably die in the violence,' said Orlando Flores, the assistant pastor there.

Pastor Flores felt that one of the most important tasks of the church in El Salvador was to prepare them to be victorious during persecution.

'We have been preparing our church here in such a way that even if they close the building, it will not affect us because we have cells already established all over the city. So if our people don't have this large centre to meet in, they will still be receiving spiritual food because of the cells. Probably, we are coming to the point when we will have to live our faith in the same way as the early church did.'

Even as we talked, the dull hellish thud of an explosion went off in the distance, then another, and another until four bombs exploded during a thirty-minute period.

Dr Aquillon could see the concern on my face and, as it was now getting dark, he volunteered to take Peter and me back to the hotel.

Feeling a little shaky, I lay quietly on the bed, thanking the Lord that I was still in one piece. Peter switched on the television and we began watching a documentary about Somalia in East Africa.

Then, a nerve-shattering blast shook the room. We both jumped instinctively off our beds, rigid with shock.

'That's a bomb,' said Peter breathlessly as I stared at him with wide, frightened eyes. 'I think they've got the hotel.'

We switched off all the lights and scanned the velvet darkness from the balcony. Smoke was curling ugly and black across the sky. I grabbed my camera and we hastened nervously to the emergency staircase. Glass was lying everywhere from windows that had been blown in.

We took the steps of the staircase two at a time and soon joined scores of people who had also rushed to see what had happened. The scene was ablaze with violence and terror. TV crews wearing tee-shirts with 'Don't shoot, I'm A Journalist' on them, appeared from the hotel bar and I joined them in picking my way through the wreckage of what had once been a lawyer's office, over the road from the hotel. Two cars had been destroyed, and a whole row of buildings had been damaged.

I stood back to survey the scene, when a well-dressed youth came over and asked me if I was a journalist. I nodded and explained I was from England.

'Would you like to know why we planted the bomb?' he asked in confidential tones, turning his rather frightening gaze on me.

I took a step backwards and nodded, not quite knowing how to react. I felt an unhealthy fascination with what he was about to tell me.

'This lawyer was on television earlier tonight criticizing the terrorists,' his eyes looked odd and white and dangerous. 'We decided to teach him a lesson and so left a package for him on his doorstep.

I was dumbstruck and gave a little defensive laugh.

'Would you like a tour of the area where we have planted other bombs in the last few days?' he continued his bizarre conversation with me. 'I'd feel honoured to show you around.'

The young man spoke perfect English and appeared to be completely sincere. I thought of those youngsters we had seen accept Christ the day before. Now here was a terrorist out in the open conducting his own propaganda campaign. He realized the importance of those 'twenty-six lead soldiers'.

I could see Peter hovering in the background desperately trying to catch my eye. 'Don't get involved,' I caught him urgently mouthing to me as I felt increasingly terrified.

'Look,' I said, my voice shrill and strident as I started to sound desperate, 'would you mind awfully if I left now? I have some urgent business back at the hotel.'

With that I turned on my heels and sprinted through the debris as fast as I could, with Peter following after me. My heart was beating too fast and my mouth was sour from the meeting. Back in the room we sank to our knees and began to pray for this young 'bomber'. We prayed for all the youth of this tragic land, that there would be a revival of God's love; that they would look for other solutions to their immense problems than that of the bomb and the bullet.

We checked out next morning and I shook hands with the same boy who had issued the 'be careful' warning on my arrival.

'God bless you,' I said, as we shook hands. 'I will pray for you.'

'Thank you,' he said wistfully. 'But not just for me. Please pray for our country. We need all your prayers.'

Jose and Manuel were to stay on, but before leaving for the airport, Peter and I went to survey the bomb damage.

'It's a mess,' said Peter as we looked at the twisted metal and charred remains of the buildings and cars that had been blasted the night before.

'This whole area of Central America is a mess. But Jesus came to heal messes!'

I met Peter several times after this trip at his home in Southern California and we began writing *Prophets of Revolution* together. While there I gained a fresh appreciation of the American people; their warmth and friendliness.

'I'd just love to move over here one day and share these lessons I have been learning from the suffering church with the Americans,' I told Peter during a break in our writing efforts. 'I just know they would respond well and want to become involved in helping these people in their plight.'

22

Blurred Images and Lebanon

Never be afraid to trust an unknown future to a known God.

CORRIE TEN BOOM

I screwed up my eyes to look at Norma, but all I could see were blurred images of her pretty face.

'Are you all right?' she asked anxiously. 'You've been screwing up your eyes and looking at me in a strange way for some days now.'

I paused for a moment then let it all pour out. 'Well, love, I didn't want to worry you but I haven't been able to see properly—and it's getting worse by the hour.'

Before she could respond, I continued my tale of woe, 'Also I keep drinking gallons of coke and then dashing to the bathroom. On top of that I've got a rash that just won't clear up.'

Without a moment's hesitation, she said, 'I think you should see the doctor, Dan. Something's radically wrong.'

I suppose I had hoped these problems would clear up, but now I was faced with what seemed like a hopeless situation. If I allowed this to continue it could only get worse, yet if I went to the doctor, he might tell me that I had an incurable disease—a 'verdict' I did not want to hear.

I finally visited my doctor and, as I described my disturbing symptoms, he decided to take a blood test.

'You have all the classic symptoms of diabetes,' he said. 'The test will tell us if you *do* have it.'

'If I *do,* does that mean I will have to inject myself with insulin?' I asked, squirming at the thought of sticking a needle into my arm several times a day.

'No, Dan,' he said gently. 'I would guess that you have what is called non-insulin-dependent or adult-onset diabetes. You won't be alone. Many millions of people suffer from this.'

But then he went on to say, 'Complications such as gangrene, kidney disease, blindness, heart attack and strokes are associated with diabetes. It is also the most likely cause of new cases of blindness.

'However, Dan, if we catch it in time, as in your case, the chances of developing these complications are greatly reduced.'

He looked at me and said that this kind of diabetes strikes mainly people over forty, especially the overweight. I was forty-two and certainly carrying more than my fair share of flab.

'You're going to have to lose quite a few pounds, and also I'll give you some medicine . . . that is if the blood test proves positive.'

It did! The laboratory discovered that I had more than three times the blood-sugar level than is normal. At first I began to be angry with God. Why should I get such an illness when I was finally in his full-time service? What possible good could come out of this?

Also, having a hearty appetite, I wasn't sure how I was going to cope with a food intake which would be one-third of what I was used to.

'Just think,' said Norma, as I half-heartedly picked at the bowl of Grape Nuts and milk set before me at breakfast, 'The Bible teaches us that our body is the temple of the Holy Spirit and once you have lost all that weight, you will have a much better temple for the Lord to dwell in.'

At first I felt an almost constant hunger, and I found my nerves often stretched to their limit. But there were compensations. My eyesight was getting better, my thirst was more normal, the skin problem was clearing up, and I began to feel that I might enjoy being skinny again— something I hadn't been for twenty years.

Then, just one week after I had been diagnosed as diabetic, I felt a frightening stabbing pain in my chest. Norma noticed my deathly white appearance as I walked through the door.

'I think I'm having a heart attack,' I winced as the pain carved up my chest.

Within thirty minutes I was in the Intensive Care unit of a local hospital, totally immobilized and attached to several machines. Heart specialists frantically checked the instruments as I was put onto an IV drip.

However, strangely enough, I felt a real peace. 'Lord,' I whispered to the accompaniment of the electronic bleeps of the cardiac monitor recording my heartbeat, 'I might be joining you very soon and I'm ready! Whatever you have in mind for me, I'll accept it.'

As I lay there, I let my mind drift back to eighteen months previously when we had packed up our lives into six suitcases and headed for Southern California full of hope and excitement for our new life.

Open Doors had invited me to spearhead a project to make the plight of the suffering church better known to Americans and to others around the world. Norma and I had put a fleece before the Lord that we would only move if our sons Andrew and Peter were in agreement. They were not committed Christians at the time, and we thought there was a good chance they would want to stay in the country of their birth.

So we asked them separately how they felt about it.

Both Andrew and Peter said they would go to the 'New World'. But still we needed final confirmation—a Scripture that pointed the way for us. So I was excited when, one morning, I was reading Isaiah 54, and verse two just 'popped up' in front of me.

I called Norma from the kitchen and read it to her: 'Enlarge the place of your tent, and let the curtains of your habitations be stretched out; hold not back, lengthen your cords and strengthen your stakes.'

'Well,' she said, a smile crossing her face, 'it seems that we are to move on yet again. Though this will be our biggest as a family.'

On hearing the news, Peter added brightly, 'California here we come!'

It was a slightly scared Wooding family that left Heathrow Airport on June 28, 1982. But after just over nine hours of flying, I could see excitement on the faces of Norma, Andrew and Peter, as our '747' approached Los Angeles.

We were met by Peter Gonzales, with whom I had co-authored *Prophets of Revolution,* and his son, Peter Junior. It was quite an experience getting acclimatized to life in the United States and launching the *Open Doors News Service,* which began with a mailing list of about 100 and is now sent each month to 1,000 newspapers and media outlets around the world.

I enjoyed the challenge of sharing the vital message of the suffering church through the American mass media, including the 700-Club, the Trinity Broadcasting Network, the Moody Radio Network and eventually, being appointed as a stringer for the UPI Radio Network which is based in Washington, DC.

But now, here I was, in the American hospital with, it seemed, my career about to come to an abrupt and tragic end. With diabetes and now heart trouble, there was no way I could continue to report from the hot spots of this world. My next assignment, to the most dangerous country on earth, Lebanon, was definitely off. I had agreed to go there with a team of doctors and paramedics organized by the Carlsbad-based group, CERT (Christian Emergency Relief Teams).

After twenty-four hours my condition stabilized and, much to my relief, I was told that I had not had a heart attack, though the illness could be linked to the massive change my body was now undergoing through diet and medication.

'I was supposed to go to Lebanon at the end of the week,' I told the doctor who had diagnosed my diabetes. 'But I've told my wife to cancel the trip.'

I nearly did have a heart attack when he told me that I was wrong in doing that.

'Dan you *should* go! You will be with expert medical people while you're there. The worse thing you can do is to consider yourself an invalid.' He exuded that traditional paternal air that you associate with a doctor.

'It's as if you've fallen off a horse. You need to get straight back on and start again.'

I didn't like to tell him that it wasn't just the diabetes that concerned me, but the mindless killing that was going on in that war-torn land. Maybe I would survive this situation, only to be cut down by a bullet or a bomb in violence-crazy Lebanon.

But I had also to consider that God had spared me from death in a bombing in El Salvador, freed me from prison in Nigeria and protected me during my time in Uganda.

So, with great trepidation, I decided I would go to Lebanon, whatever the consequences . . . .

The fourteen-year-old crippled Lebanese boy manoeuvred himself on his crutches towards me, then stopped in his tracks and held out his hand.

'Welcome,' he said in faltering English, adding with a faint smile, 'You like my gun?' With that he gestured towards the pistol secured in a holster at his side.

I smiled weakly, not quite knowing how to respond. I really shouldn't have been surprised. This was southern Lebanon in the summer of 1983, where almost everyone owned at least one firearm and twenty private armies operated apparently at will.

To one of the team, Dr Tom Suard, Lebanon was all quite a shock, despite the fact that he regularly treated knife and gunshot wounds resulting from gang warfare in LA ghettos. 'Working in the hospital in Los Angeles, we are rather detached,' said the doctor who was just starting out on his medical career. 'They bring the injured in and we take care of them. We're not out in the field. We don't have the bombs bursting. We're not on the cutting edge. We're well protected. Lebanon is like being on the frontline.'

Tom was one of a unique team of twenty doctors, paramedics, and pastors whom I had joined in this 'invasion' of southern Lebanon as part of a love-strike to a country that has seen little but hate over the previous few years. Each individual had raised a good deal of money to cover the cost of the trip which was also organized in conjunction with Lebanon Aid, an organization started shortly after the Israelis invaded Lebanon in June 1982.

The group split up into four teams of medics and pastors, and each was to work in villages and cities treating the sick and also presenting the gospel to all who would listen. Some worked with Lebanon Aid medical vans, others in more permanent clinics.

The medics diagnosed what was wrong, administered what treatment they could, then prayed with each patient. At the same time they kept an eye on my condition, but, fortunately, my health held out.

The most experienced doctor in the party, John Merriman, said, 'The Lebanese we saw didn't have any war-related injuries except stress. We could see the manifestations of stress in people'.

The widespread stress was not really surprising, as it

was estimated that at that time the civil war between Lebanese Christians and Muslims had claimed more than 30,000 lives. (And that was on top of the 19,000 killed in the fighting in the past twelve months between Israel and the Palestine Liberation Organization.)

Dr Merriman and Dr Suard presented two extremes of background and experience on this Lebanon mission. Dr Merriman was widely travelled. He had been on short-term medical missions to Central America, including Guatemala, while Tom Suard, on the other hand, had never been overseas before.

Both, however, had the same aim: to bring some of Christ's love to this ravaged land. And to all participants, Lebanon was a land of surprises. In some ways it was like the Wild West except, tragically, much of the killing was taking place in the name of God. It still is a country where the different brands of Christianity and Islam, led by their armed feudal chieftains, try to outdo each other with their vile atrocities.

One CERT team was kidnapped, taken to a Christian Falangist meeting, and then subjected to propaganda. 'It was something out of a James Bond film,' one paramedic told me. 'We were all put in a vehicle and driven there at speeds of up to 70 miles per hour.

'When we got to the meeting we found the area heavily guarded. They made sure that nobody was following us, and then we went into the meeting. There were guns lying around everywhere, while others had them hidden in their clothing.'

Several of us, on one occasion, got another insight into the situation. A Lebanese doctor took us into the desperately dangerous Shouf mountains. The doctor ministered his medicine in villages controlled by the mystical Druse sect (a group derived from Islam but differing strongly from it). We were the first westerners to enter the area in ten years. 'I'm probably the only Christian who could come out of this area alive,' the doctor told us as an armed

Druse militia-man checked us out as we sat in our vehicles high in the mountains.

The doctor later told me, 'I know there is so much hatred in my country, but I can only follow the example of Jesus who showed love and reconciliation to all. Love is the only answer to the problem of this time.'

The CERT team soon realized that the real long-term answer to Lebanon's problems is a spiritual one. So in both small and larger ways the team members tried to share the gospel with all whom they came in contact with.

Mike Landrum, a medical student, kept it simple. He had a Gideon Bible with him in which John 3:16 was printed in Arabic. 'We were in a predominately Muslim village,' he told me. 'I took out that little Bible and showed the verse to some men waiting to be seen by the doctor. They read it out loud. It was a tremendously rewarding thing for me to just stand and watch them read that verse of Scripture. It was the best I could do.'

Jon Courson, a pastor of Jacksonville Calvary Chapel in Oregon, was able to reach out to a wider audience through an interpreter. He addressed several home meetings and one day spoke near a medical van to a large crowd of villagers. Many accepted Christ during his meetings.

Lebanon Aid had been taking in more teams of pastors from Great Britain and the United States. They were encouraged to stay for a few weeks and live in Lebanese homes.

'Southern Lebanon is wide open for the gospel at this time,' said Bible teacher Mac Kingsbury from England. We met him as he was going house-to-house in both Christian and Muslim villages. 'There is a great hunger here and people respond readily to love. They have been so starved of it over the past few years. I would definitely encourage others to come here, not so much to do Bible teaching, but evangelism.'

Nasr Audi, former Chief Deputy to the speaker of the

Lebanese Parliament and then President of Lebanon Aid, said that there had never been a better time for Christians to take Arabic Bibles into southern Lebanon.

Nasr told me that he had committed his life to Jesus Christ as the war between Israel and the PLO raged in his country. He was led to Christ by Ray Barnett, who had just started Lebanon Aid in the country.

'Many people here were like me. They believed they were Christian because they belonged to what is called a Christian family,' said Nasr. 'But they have to realize, like I did, that what is needed is a personal relationship with Jesus Christ. And the best way they can get to know him is through the Bible.'

Nasr said that most 'Christian' Lebanese do not own a Bible. 'They leave it to the local priest to interpret the Scriptures for them. We have already been able to place 2,500 Bibles, but that is hardly scratching the surface,' he continued. 'There are some 580,000 people in southern Lebanon, and I would like to see each one of them own a Bible.'

The director of CERT, David Courson, said that this trip showed something very important to the people of Lebanon. 'Jesus instructed us to come and heal in his name. This is what I believe we have been able to do in a small way,' he declared. 'There is a saying we have in CERT: "People don't care how much you know until they see how much you care."'

The whole experience of Lebanon was totally faith-building for me, because I realized that my predicament was relatively minor compared with the Lebanese.

I also began to realize that we are called to be servants —whatever the cost may be to us. We are not called to be whining complainers, something I had become for a short time. Our example was Jesus himself.

Since first discovering that blurred vision is not always bad, I have learned to be more dependent on Jesus and, much to Norma's delight, I've lost quite a portion of the old Dan Wooding. In fact, I'm over four stone lighter.

'I guess that day my vision went fuzzy really did help me to get my faith more directly in focus,' I shared with Norma recently.

She smiled quietly to herself, opened her Bible and read to me a verse that the Lord had given her from Jeremiah 18:6: 'Behold like the clay in the potter's hand, so are you in my hand.'

She turned her watery eyes on mine and said, 'When I first read this you were still in the hospital. It's as if the Lord was saying, "Don't worry, everything is going to be fine. I'm just doing some remodelling in Dan's life."'

Then looking at me, she grinned, 'So far I think he's done a very good job . . . . I think you must be the first person to emigrate to America and lose weight!'

As an added confirmation from the Lord that I should continue with my 'twenty-six lead soldiers', despite my illness, I heard the following year that the article I wrote for the California magazine *Contemporary Christian* on the Lebanon trip—'Bibles & Bandages'—won first prize in the reporting section of the Evangelical Press Association (of the USA) in its 'Higher Goals' contest.

It began to seem to me as if the needs of our Christian brethren were never-ending and my work with the *Open Doors News Service* meant my bags were always packed ready for the next assignment. Soon I would be on my way to Central America, this time to Honduras where I would be meeting a special brand of people, the Miskito Indians.

And the Lord gave Norma and me a special bonus, for both Andrew and Peter became committed Christians in California. Andrew returned to Europe and spent eighteen months in England with Youth With a Mission in 1985 and has also studied at Capernwray Hall Bible College in Carnforth. Peter became the editor of his high school newspaper and is now studying journalism at college.

23

Fine by God's Grace

The real problem is not why some pious, humble, believing people suffer, but why some do not.

C.S. LEWIS

'Save the bell, save the bell,' screamed the distraught Miskito women as the whooping and yelling Sandinista soldiers torched their church.

As the fire took hold on their Moravian sanctuary close to the Honduras border in Nicaragua, men from the village dashed into the blazing church and climbed up the bell tower. Despite the choking smoke and flames, they were able to dismantle the precious bell and bring it down to safety.

As they dragged the rusty old bell away from the devastation, the bell tower suddenly collapsed and crashed unceremoniously to the ground.

By now every house in their village was also ablaze. Possessions were destroyed, Bibles and hymnals were charred ruins, cattle lay dead in the streets after being shot by the soldiers who were moving on to the next village for another 'scorched earth' campaign of terror against these peace-loving Indians.

'We carried the bell eleven miles to the Honduras border and then a further thirty miles to this refugee camp,' said a Miskito woman in the Mocoron Camp.

Now that very bell was being used to call the mainly Evangelical Miskitos to worship. It was a defiant symbol of their courage and faith in the face of great persecution by the Marxist Sandinista government which, during 1981, saw the arrest of some 253 of their leaders, including ten Moravian pastors and 140 elders. They also imprisoned many of the village and tribal leaders of this traditionally peaceful and industrious people. Some were eventually released but at least 130 were sentenced to prison for terms ranging up to twenty years for their alleged part in the incident that was dubbed as the 'Red Christmas Plot'.

There are an estimated 125,000 Miskitos, who have for centuries preserved its distinctiveness. They have inhabited the largely desolate Atlantic Coast region, earning their living mainly as hunters and fishermen. That was until the Sandinistas moved against them. Under the Sandinistas' rule the Miskitos have come to experience what one Nicaraguan journalist described as 'the worst cultural dislocation in centuries'.

I had flown in the Spring of 1984 to Tegucigalpa, the Honduran capital, and then by small plane to the Mocoron camp to visit these Miskito Indians (the name is derived from 'mosquito'—they infest that region).

Leading our team was the Reverend Tom Claus, a member of the Turtle clan of Mohawks from Six Nations Reserve near Branton, Ontario, and president of CHIEF (Christian Hope Indian Eskimo Fellowship), based in Phoenix, Arizona. Claus was making his third visit to the Miskitos. He had already, through Indian Christians in North America, provided them with blankets, lanterns, tools, housing, food, Bibles in the Miskito language, musical instruments and hymnals, but this time he was bearing communion sets to be used by 1,000 of these Indians at a time. (Also in the group was Totonac Indian

leader, Manuel Arenas who heads up the Totonac Bible
Centre in La Union, Mexico.)

As we stood in the camp surrounded by many of the
smiling Miskito pastors, who took turns in hugging us,
Claus told me why he had brought the communion sets.

'On my last visit to the camp, I asked the Miskitos to tell
me the one thing they most wanted,' explained Claus.
'They answered, "We would like to celebrate the Lord's
Supper. Could you bring us communion sets for at least
1,000 people? We will take turns in using them."

'Even in their desperate need for clothes, food and
shelter, their first thought was worship and devotion to
their heavenly Father. I was touched by their sincere desire to fellowship in God's presence.'

Claus nearly wept when, the day after our arrival,
Pastor Nabut Zacharias, a Moravian minister, called his
believers together for their first communion service since
they fled Nicaragua some two years previously.

He chose a spot on the banks by the Mocoron River and
his flock turned over their dugout canoes to use as pews.
Old and young alike solemnly remembered the Lord's
Supper against the backdrop of the jungle river-life. As I
stood observing this moving occasion, I let my mind
wander back to the little wooden mission hall in
Birmingham's Sparkbrook district where my father had
'broken bread' with his small flock. This couldn't have
been more different, yet we all belonged to the same
'body'.

Claus told the Miskitos, 'I'm an Indian and so your pain
is my pain; your suffering is my suffering and I want my
people in the United States and Canada to help bear your
burden at this time.

'But more than that. Jesus is bearing your burden and
he is representing you before the Father. You are not
deserted; you are not alone before the Father. You are
not deserted; you are not alone because we Christians of
North America want to stand with you, and we know God

is with you.

'In your suffering we want you to know that there are
many of us who care, so cast your cares on us, and on the
Lord, for we care deeply for you.'

Suffering is something these Indians know intimately.
One of the worst atrocities took place in December 1981,
in the village of Cruce de las Balsas, which was one of the
many that the Sandinistas, anxious to strengthen their
borders, designated as part of a 120-mile 'military zone'.
The soldiers began forcibly expelling the Indians and
force-marching men, women, the weak, the aged, and
children, south through the jungles for eleven to fifteen
days, to what Tom Claus described as 'concentration
camps'.

'The soldiers came in looking for blood,' said one pastor
as tears welled up in his eyes. 'They buried alive thirty-five
of our men. They just left them as we stood helplessly by
until they had suffocated and died.' There was one sur-
vivor, a teenager, who managed to claw his way out of
the covered-in hole. As he staggered away, he was shot at
by the Sandinistas and hit in the arm. He was in the
Mocoron Camp when I arrived there, but with only one
arm.

A Miskito mother described the scene when she and her
family tried to cross the Coco River which divides
Nicaragua and Honduras.

'We were paddling our dugout canoe across the river
when the Sandinista soldiers took aim at us,' said the
mother, her eyes still conveying the horror of that time. 'I
let out a scream as my little girl was shot, then my husband. Two more of my children were cut down by the
soldiers' bullets.'

Within seconds, a family of four Christian Miskitos flee-
ing their homeland had been murdered by the Sandinistas.
Their boat sank and the mother, clutching her remaining
child, managed to swim to the bank, leaving the bullet-
riddled bodies of the others to float down the river and out

to sea.

Professor Bernard Nietschmann, who in 1983 spent two-and-a-half months with the Miskitos, gave the following report about the denial of religious freedom to the Miskitos:

'Only in those villages now under the protection of Miskito warriors (anti-Sandinista rebels) are religous services being held. For some villages I visited, that protection had only recently been secured. And even in this large zone many villages cannot hold church services because their religous leaders are in jail or in exile in Honduras or Costa Rica.

'During the Sandinista military occupations of villages, churches have commonly been used as jails, to detain men and women accused or suspected of counter-revolutionary activities. Churches have also been used to house the Sandinista soldiers. Bibles and hymn books have been destroyed. Villagers accuse the Sandinista soldiers of defecating and urinating in the churches. There are many credible reports of these activities. I heard reports of churches that had been burned elsewhere in Indian communities, but in the areas I visited I saw no churches that had been destroyed.

'The Miskitos are a very religious people, and they have suffered greatly from the denial of their freedom of religion. In almost all of my discussions with hundreds of Miskito men and women, this was a principal grievance they reported to me.'

In October 1983, Bernard Nietschmann, who is also an American geographer to the human rights commission of the Organization of American States, gave a sweeping description of the Sandinistas' mistreatment of the Miskitos. Nietschmann, who many believe to be the world's leading outside authority on the Miskito Indians, said after his two-and-a-half months inside their territories that he had found 'widespread, systematic and arbitrary human rights violations by the Sandinista government including arbitrary killings, arrests and interrogations; rapes; torture; continuing forced relocations of village populations; destruction of villages; restriction and prohibition of freedom of travel: prohibition of village food production; restriction and denial of any access to basic and necessary store foods; the complete absence of any medicine, health care, or educational services; the denial of religious freedom; and the looting of households and sacking of villages'.

While at Mocoron I was told that despite the dangers, the Miskitos were continuing to head for the safety of Honduras from their traditional homeland in the rain forests and swamps.

While at the camp I discovered that more than 25,000 Miskitos had crossed into Honduras. Included were the much-publicized 1,000 refugees—men, women and children—who on December 24, 1983, succeeded in crossing the border after an exhausting march of three days and nights during which they were attacked, fired at by machine guns, and bombarded by the Sandinista army.

An eighty-one-year-old man, Pablo Smith, with gnarled hands and a leathery face, gathered some of his forty grandchildren around him and told me their incredible escape story in his pidgin English, a legacy of British control of the coast in the last century. It seems that Pablo was something of a Pied Piper in helping lead their dash for freedom from the Sandinistas.

'We had a total of ninety children, forty of them my own grandchildren, when we began our escape two years ago from Nicaragua,' he began. 'As we set off, we could see our villages burning. They were all destroyed. Nothing was left. They killed our pigs and cattle as well. The soldiers just sprayed them with machine-gun fire after burning down our homes.

'For the first few hours we walked up to our waists in mud. It was terrible. Some of the women were suckling their babies and were so weak they would fall over into the mud.

'Finally, we came to the Savannah, an old Indian trail, and it was much easier. It took us a total of three days and nights to get to Mocoron. We are grateful to God that we are here and we believe God will continue to help us.'

The first thing they did when they arrived was not to construct homes, but to pitch in and build churches so they could worship together again.

The Miskitos were first evangelized by Moravian missionaries from Europe in the nineteenth century. They have a heritage of evangelical belief.

'Partly for that reason, but also because of differences in language and race, the Marxist-dominated Sandinista government considers them a threat to the progress of its left-wing social reforms,' said Dr Dale W. Kietzman, President of World Literature Crusade and a respected Indian anthropologist.

Dr Kietzman noted that the Miskito Indians were now coming across the border from much further inland than earlier groups who fled into Honduras. 'The situation for the young Miskitos is especially desperate. They have left because they do not feel they will have any chance for a proper education in Nicaragua,' he added. 'Being labelled as "counter-revolutionaries" is only the latest in a long history of discrimination against these Indian Christians by their Spanish-speaking countrymen, but it certainly does not shake their Christian faith.'

Tim Goble, president of Fellowship of World Christians, a California-based ministry providing spiritual and material help, told me that the suffering these Indians had undergone had caused a real spiritual awakening among them.

Goble was making his third trip to Mocoron, the hub of the refugee camps in eastern Honduras. 'Of course,' he said, 'many of these refugees are Christians. In fact, they are here because they were unwilling to compromise their Christian faith with the Marxist government in their homeland (Nicaragua). But some of the people's faith back then had grown cold and dry; now they are really getting on fire!'

Goble cited the growing number of early-morning prayer meetings as an indicator of spiritual renewal. 'Many of the refugee churches start ringing their chimes (usually a small piece of iron) at 4 a.m., calling the people to gather for prayer. This goes on every morning, and the churches are usually packed out.

'The refugee churches are overflowing at their Sunday services. One church I spoke at was so full they had all the children leave. One of our short-term team members who spoke Spanish held an impromptu Sunday School class for them. Still there were people standing outside looking in.'

Furthermore his volunteers had built a trading post and added an emergency room to the hospital at Mocoron. 'Contact with these men is a real blessing to the refugees, as well as an encouragement to the relief workers,' he said.

'When we were getting ready to depart, the team came to me and said they wanted to leave all their tools with the church I had spoken in that Sunday morning, to help them build a larger place of worship. The pastor accepted the tools with tears in his eyes. You just can't beat that kind of love and encouragement.'

Goble then related an incident that took place when walking back with a Miskito pastor from an early-morning prayer meeting.

'I asked him if they prayed like this when they were in Nicaragua. He shook his head and said, "No . . . if we had, maybe we wouldn't be here now."'

If I needed any further evidence of the deeply-held faith of these Indians, I received it when I asked one of the Miskitos how he was. 'Fine, by God's grace,' was his firm reply. It is the answer all Miskitos give to that question. Despite all that has happened to them, they are still 'fine, by God's grace'.

A lesson to us all!

24

'The Greater the Sorrow, the Closer Is God'

If everyone had remained silent we might well have been dead.

GEORGI VINS, ONCE A CHRISTIAN PRISONER IN THE GULAG

Military music blared loudly from the radio in our compartment of the Trans-Siberian Express. We were leaving Moscow's Yaroslavl Station, to begin the world's longest railway journey: to and then across Siberia.

It was February 1985, and I was there to research an article for the *Open Doors News Service*. I would be travelling 3,200 miles in freezing winter conditions—and that is only half way across the enormous expanses of Siberia, a waste land where up to two million Soviets have been sent to labour camps for a variety of reasons ranging from criminal to political to religious. It is an area that is larger in size than either China or the United States.

Down the length of this snake-like, electric train, Russians, Georgians, Siberians, Americans and British started unpacking their belongings from battered suitcases and began to turn their two, four and six-bed compartments into temporary homes. Yuri, an over-sized friendly bear of a man, just a few compartments back, started to

214

peel off his heavy clothes and put on the blue pyjama jacket he would wear for the rest of the trip. Others, in different compartments, began unravelling packages containing loaves of bread, hunks of cheese and generous supplies of vodka.

'I think I'm going to enjoy this after all,' commented one of our group of travellers consisting of ten Americans and one British exile. I had joined them for this two-week visit to the Soviet Union, actually surprised I had been granted a visa after the 'Road Block to Moscow' incident back in 1972.

The journey had got off to an unusual start. For as we stood at the wind-blown Moscow station waiting for our luggage to be loaded on board, fists had flown furiously just a few yards away as two porters, dressed like grizzly bears, exchanged blows for the privilege of loading the baggage.

With hostilities finally ending—not without bloodshed—the warring porters were separated by their colleagues, and we were finally allowed to board the *Rossiya* (Russia) express. We settled into our two-berth, first-class compartments (yes, there is a class system even in the supposedly classless society of the Soviet Union), and although not large, they were actually quite comfortable, each with upholstered berths, a table, mirror, radio, heating (or air conditioning in the summer), and an attendant-call button.

As we plunged deeper and deeper into the frozen wastes of Siberia, I stood in the corridor, staring out of the window, watching the full moon, and reflecting on the case of the Vashchenko and Chymkhalov families. They had made the reverse journey in June 1978 from their home in the coal-mining town of Chernogorsk, 2,000 miles east of Moscow. This group of Siberian Pentecostalists who were to play a great role in my own life, wanted to emigrate from the Soviet Union so they could practise their faith free from the persecution of communist authorities.

Their date with fate was June 27, 1978. In the party wanting freedom was Peter Vashchenko, a man of medium height in his mid-fifties, with dark hair and moustache, and wearing a neat dark suit. Among the 150,000 Pentecostals living in the Soviet Union, Peter had been a leading advocate of religious freedom since 1960. At his side were his wife, fair-haired Augustina, and four of their children, Lida, Lyuba, Lilia and John. Another boy, Timothy, came with his mother, Maria Chymkhalov.

The costs of being a Christian in Siberia were high for the Vashchenkos. Lida, especially, suffered terribly. Her family insisted on bringing her up as a Christian and did not want to send her to the local school where atheism was taught. So her father made a secret place for the children to hide in. 'Sometimes the police would make lightning searches,' she recalled. 'When they came at night our hearts were beating so loudly that it seemed they would hear us upstairs. If they came at daytime, we would hide there frozen with terror. The memory of it makes me shiver all over.'

For five long months, despite constant searches by the police, Peter was able to keep the secret. Then one day a police car came by and the officers caught the children playing in front of the house. Someone had forgotten to keep lookout. Lida ran into the barn and scrambled away under a large wooden box, but was discovered. 'A policeman jumped on my leg and finally grabbed me. I screamed and then the rest came and took me.'

Lida, then eleven, was placed for a while in the Abakan State Orphanage—the home of runaways, orphans and outlaws. 'It was a very difficult period of my life. I did not try to find friends, because I spent my days in secret loneliness and in tears. For me it was if I had been buried alive.'

Then again, when she was seventeen, Lida was taken from her parents, along with her three younger sisters,

Lyuba, Nadaya and Vera, and placed in another children's home. Her parents were imprisoned in Moscow because they had tried again to talk to the Americans about their planned emigration to the USA. Peter was imprisoned for one year and underwent investigations in a psychiatric hospital. Augustina was imprisoned for more than two years.

'After a brief stay in the state-owned children's home in Krasnoyarsk,' said Lida, 'we were sent to Kansk. We were taken to the plane in a special vehicle escorted by police. When the plane arrived at Kansk airport, a security truck was waiting near the exit. There were comments from astonished people such as, "What kind of children can they be, to be in the hands of the police?"

'But how could they know who we really were? What criminal needs six to eight policemen to keep him at bay? Many times during my twenty-seven years under Soviet control I have had a police escort, but I still can't get used to it. Every time I am surrounded by police, I feel ashamed and want to cry, "Listen, all of you! Don't look at me like that! I'm not a criminal. I haven't earned your reproachful glances and degrading comments." But then I think of Jesus Christ, and I am reminded that he didn't *want* to answer, not that he had *no* answer. He knew that his questioners were interested neither in the questions nor in the answers. They wanted to sentence him, not only by their questions, but also by distorting his answers.'

Employment for Lida was always a problem. As a Christian, she was a marked person for the authorities. For instance, when she was just twenty-four years old, she refused a position as a store superintendent, because it involved giving lectures on atheism to the staff. Instead, she went to work as an orderly in a maternity hospital in Chernogorsk. Across the street was a women's aid service and a place where abortions were carried out daily by the state. Sometimes babies which had been aborted late and had survived would be carried across to the hospital. Although they were fed, they were not placed in the intensive care unit. Naturally it was heartbreaking for Lida to care for such 'tortured babies'.

One day in 1975, Lida asked if she could look after one of the aborted babies who had survived. She took the baby which she named Aaron home and cared for him and eventually legally adopted him. When Aaron was just five months old, the authorities took the baby back for medical experiments.

'They got the mother to agree to experimental surgery on his brain and also to test new drugs,' said Lida. 'Normally, they would do this type of experimenting on animals, but they chose to do it on Aaron instead.

'When he died, they buried him in a local cemetery and I went there to dig him up to get the evidence about the way he was killed.'

This was just another example of the intentional cruelty the authorities levelled at Christians in the Soviet Union.

So it was not surprising that the single-minded Vashchenkos had been trying to emigrate since 1962. An attempt to discuss their emigration with US officials in 1978 was to be frustrated. Despite the fact that Peter was clutching a letter from the embassy inviting him to come and discuss his family emigration, the Russian guards would not let them through. As a heated discussion ensued, the guards began to beat sixteen-year-old John with their clubs.

While this was happening the rest of the family ran past the surprised guards and took refuge in the lobby of the embassy.

'We ran like we were escaping from a wild beast,' Lida told me. 'For we knew that if we were caught it would be prison and maybe even death. As we ran we kept shouting at the top of our voices, "Help! Help!"'

'When we first arrived, they tried different ways to persuade us to leave the embassy, but we knew that leaving would be death for us.

'Then, an official at the embassy made a list and hung it on the wall saying that if volunteers would like to feed us, would they please sign up. So each day these kind people would bring us food. It was a different family each day.'

Eventually, the embassy co-operated with them and gave them a basement room to live in. They all lived in a cramped twelve feet by twenty feet room behind the embassy barber shop. They could look out through the iron grill at the booted feet of the Soviet guards and beyond to the grinding traffic of Moscow's Tchaikovsky Street.

So began what was to be one of the longest 'sit-ins' in history. It was a gesture that was to strike at the very heart of the Kremlin. The 'Seven' became something of a worldwide *cause célèbre,* with marches and vigils taking place around the world for them.

I was told of their case during a visit to Seattle when I met with Dr Kent Hill, a history professor at Seattle Pacific University in the spring of 1981. 'Dan, I was in Moscow at the time they rushed into the American Embassy and they became my close friends,' Hill, a fluent Russian speaker who had worked for their release for years, told me at his home. 'They are wonderful people whom I spent many hours with. I speak Russian and we would have Bible studies together.

'Could you launch a campaign on their behalf in England? There is a stalemate. It seems the US and Russians are just not talking to each other on this case. Maybe if a third country got involved, that could break the stalemate.'

Those few words were the challenge that launched the 'Campaign to Free the Siberian Seven', which mobilized thousands of British Christians to action on behalf of these seven courageous Christians.

When I returned to England, I shared Hill's challenge with Peter Meadows, Publishing Director of *Buzz* magazine, Tony Collins, then editor at Hodder & Stoughton, and Danny Smith, a journalist friend, who was to spearhead the campaign in Britain.

Within weeks, the campaign had been launched, thousands had signed a petition on their behalf at Spring Harvest, a Christian convention, and more than 100 Members of Parliament and the House of Lords had pledged their support to the cause. Trafalgar Square was packed with demonstrators on behalf of the Siberians.

I joined American and British Christians in leading a long march of 3,000 people through London to the Soviet Embassy in Kensington Palace Gardens, London, where an all-night vigil took place.

There were press conferences, badges, petitions, rallies, but most of all, there was prayer. The campaign spread around the world from Britain and even returned to the United States where thousands of American Christians showed their solidarity with the 'Siberian Seven'.

But still the Kremlin showed no compassion—until Augustina began a hunger-strike on Christmas Day, 1981, and Lida began her twenty-eight day fast shortly afterwards. Their actions finally captured world headlines and began the incredible turn-around in the Kremlin's thinking towards these seven Christians. The Soviets began to worry about the bad publicity a death in the embassy would cause. Especially harmful to them was an article which appeared in *Time* magazine which was headlined 'Deadly Game in a US Embassy, Soviet Pentacostalists try to win freedom with a hunger strike.'

Lida was desperately ill when she was finally taken from the embassy—in the glare of the world's press—to Moscow's Botkin Hospital. After her life was saved by Soviet doctors during fourteen days in hospital, she was sent back to her home in Chernogorsk, to be, once again, reunited with her other eleven brothers and sisters.

Lida made it clear that she did not desire to risk her life. 'It was a fast to ask the Lord to intercede on our behalf,' she said.

Lida felt this 'two-pronged' strategy really paid off. 'I

knew that many non-Christians would not understand the fast "to the Lord" but would understand the hunger-strike aspect. And they did! Many politicians understood the word "hunger-strike" and paid attention to what was happening.'

Lida described the pathos in the embassy before she was carried out. 'I got on my knees and began praying. Those around me began to feel this might be the last time they would see me. So they began to ask for forgiveness for anything they may have done against me.

'I looked up at them and smiled weakly. They all seemed to be towering above me. I just wanted to pray, but they all wanted my forgiveness. I was kneeling on the floor and they just kept asking for forgiveness!'

When Lida was transported home to Chernogorsk in February, 1982, it was ironically a KGB officer who helped her.

'As I walked from the plane down the stairway, I was still very light-headed and my head started spinning and I almost fainted,' she recalled.

'It was a KGB man who held me up. I think he was afraid that I would fall over and then the world would say that they had injured me.'

When she got to her home, it was a difficult time at first for her.

'The little children didn't recognize me because I looked so different,' recalled Lida. 'I think they were a little scared of how I looked. But next day they got braver and began asking among themselves who I was. Soon they began following me everywhere—even to the bathroom! They'd stand at the door and wait until I came out.

'If I went to lie down on the bed, they would sit down on my bed and just look at me. Often I would lie there so weak and fall asleep and they would throw their arms and legs about me and go to sleep too.'

One extraordinary fact that Lida revealed was that when she returned to Chernogorsk, she made an

American flag with thirteen stars (that's all the material she could get hold of), and put it on the roof of their home.

'Whenever the KGB came to try and pull it down, our Alsatian dog would go for them,' she smiled. 'We wanted to show them that we still wanted to emigrate and that we believed that America was the home of the free.'

Eventually, the prayers and campaigning paid off, and Lida was freed in April, 1983. On June 27, fifteen members of the Vashchenko family were allowed to leave for the West, followed shortly afterwards by fifteen members of the Chymkhalov family, including Maria and Timothy. They clutched Russian Bibles given out by their American supporters and one of them wore a T-shirt with the Bible verse inscribed on it, 'If God is for us, who can be against us?'

Martyn Halsall of *The Guardian,* said, 'When I saw Peter Vashchenko coming down the steps of the plane in Vienna, I was surprised to see how small he was. A small man in a crumpled brown suit, smiling, because he had taken on the Soviet government and won.'

All have settled in the United States, though Peter has since died from cancer.

After Lida arrived in the West, she first of all headed for Israel. It was there that I first met her. We stood together as she gazed wistfully onto the pond-like surface of the Sea of Galilee. Suddenly her taut face creased into a broad smile.

Then I asked her if over the past five years her personal relationship with God had deepened. She answered, 'We have a hymn in Russia which says, "The greater the sorrow, the closer is God."'

I again gazed out of the window, at the frozen expanses reflected in the moonlight and felt closer to the Christians of Siberia—and closer to God!

Great happiness came to Lida on August 2, 1986, when

she married Egyptian Christian George Gergis whom she met at an English class in California, where she now lives. I attended her wedding and we live just around the corner from her new home.

25

'Transylvania, Home of Count Dracula and The Lord's Army

This is my commandment, That ye love one another, as I have loved you.

JESUS CHRIST

A full moon hung ominously in the sky over the gloomy Romanian border post on Hungary's boundary at the edge of the mysterious region of Transylvania. It was eight months since my trip to Siberia, and now I had returned to Eastern Europe on a reporting assignment for the *Open Doors News Service*. The surly Romanian guard looked suspiciously at me and said in a heavy expressionless voice, 'Do you have guns or Bibles?' I shrugged in a non-committal way as he began roughly searching through my belongings.

'It's interesting that they would put guns in the same category as Bibles,' I remarked to David, my travelling companion. 'They obviously have a great fear of God's word in this country.'

I had already read about how the Romanian authorities had recycled into toilet paper some 20,000 Hungarian Bibles shipped into Transylvania by the World Reformed Alliance in the United States in the late 1970s and 1980s.

At that time, in an attempt to placate US criticism of its violations of religious rights, the Romanian government had consented to the shipment of these Bibles to the Reformed Church in Transylvania, whose membership was ethnically Hungarian. The scandal came to light when rolls of toilet paper, on which fragments of Bible verses were still legible, reached the USA from Romania.

As we waited for the check to be completed, I wondered how Brother Andrew must have felt as he had crossed numerous borders in his now-famous blue Volkswagen with Bibles. It must have been a lonely, yet inspiring, experience for him as God blinded the eyes of the guards.

Our nerve-racking check was over and nothing had been discovered. We were about to enter Transylvania, the land of Count Dracula, and some of the world's most committed Christians.

Like Brother Jacob, a leader of The Lord's Army, an evangelical break-off from the Romanian Orthodox Church. The Orthodox Church claims about seventeen million of the nation's 23.5 million population, but this underground leader turned out to be one of Transylvania's most unusual evangelists. This 'soldier for the Lord' uses what has become known as 'Wedding Evangelism' as a way to win non-Christians to Christ in this Communist country.

'We seem to have so many weddings these days,' he chuckled as he explained how weddings have become a wonderful way to present Christ to outsiders.

'Each wedding starts around mid-day on a Saturday and continues through to midnight, with greetings being brought to the bride and groom from the Apostles Paul and Peter. We read these greetings direct from their letters found in the Bible. Sometimes we go right through the night until the following afternoon, though often we will let people get some sleep.'

He added: 'This happy occasion means we can share the

love of Christ with those there and also teach the Scriptures.'

I wondered if there were couples who went through the marriage ceremony several times to facilitate the meeting together of The Lord's Army? He smiled and said nothing.

Dors, the Army's leader, knows all about persecution. Seventeen of his more than seventy years have been spent in prison for his faith and most of his 'free' years he has been under virtual house arrest. He predicts that there will be more persecution for The Lord's Army very shortly, and urges Western Christians to pray for them.

'I don't ask them to pray that we will avoid it,' he says. 'On the contrary, it is our lot. Pray that we can endure and take advantage of the opportunities for witness that only intense persecution brings.'

Dors has described the Army as 'an evangelical movement of renewal and living in Christ'. He said that he did not know exactly how many members they had. 'At a rough guess,' he declared, 'the number would be somewhere between 500,000 and 1,000,000.'

Because of the incredible pressures on believers in this beautiful land bordered by the USSR, Hungary, Yugoslavia and Bulgaria, it was imperative that David and I did not cause any danger to the Christians we visited. So much of the reporting I did had to be under cover of darkness.

One evening, David and I parked our car in a turn-off close to a village. Because of the energy problems the country was experiencing, we knew that no street lights would be operating. We had memorized the believer's name and address and after a few heart-stopping minutes of walking to the edge of the village, we darted down the street where he lived and into his courtyard. His startled wife saw us and we clasped her hands together in praying fashion and she smiled brightly and ushered us into her home.

The walls of the house were covered with pictures of Jesus as she welcomed us in and then introduced us to her husband, a tiny elderly man with thick stubble on his face. He clasped us close and kissed us on both cheeks. Although neither of us spoke the other's language, we began exchanging verses by pointing them out to each other in our Bibles.

Each time he read our verse aloud, his face lit up and he pointed his finger heavenwards. Soon he began whistling hymns to us. His son came into the room and produced a Romanian-English dictionary and with the help of this we were soon conversing. As we enjoyed fellowship together, a feast was suddenly spread before us and we had the privilege of sharing a meal with these wonderful Romanian Christians. What made this spread of eggs and meat so extraordinary and generous was that since 1981 basic foodstuff, such as bread, flour, meat, eggs, sugar and oil, had been rationed.

A highlight for us came when we met with Paul Negrut and Nicholea Gheorghita, pastors of the Second Baptist Church of Oradea, the largest Baptist church in Romania (and Europe).

Dr 'Nick', a medical doctor for twenty-four years who had given up his practice to work with the church, beamed with joy as he told us how they had just baptized fifty-four converts from Billy Graham's historic visit to the church. In September 1985, Billy Graham had been in Romania for an eleven-day preaching mission and was the first American evangelist to be allowed into the country since the Communist Revolution in 1944. The pastors told us they had cleared out all of the pews from the sanctuary and some 7,000 people stood and listened to the gospel being clearly presented, and an additional 36,000 milled around outside and listened through loudspeakers.

The church, which the authorities have been trying to demolish since 1984—they have already demolished many churches in the country including three of the historic

Orthodox sites in Bucharest—faced a crisis in September 1981, when its pastor, Josif Ton, was expelled from the country. Many felt that the work would crumble when Josif left.

'What is so wonderful,' Dr Nick smiled, 'is that God has continued to bless us, and since Josif left we have had the privilege of baptizing some 700 people.'

We joined with the congregation of 3,000 for the Sunday morning service which began at 8.30 a.m. and continued through until 12.15 p.m. The sanctuary seated only about 1,500 and so the rest stood for the whole period of worship.

Travelling around Transylvania, it soon became obvious that the dreaded Secret Police, Securitate, are very active in the region, as they are in the rest of the country. This police group, among the most brutal in the whole of Eastern Europe, seemed to particularly enjoy photographing my companion and me.

Attacks on Christians, and repressive measures against defenders of religious rights, are being stepped up in Romania. Measures ranging from the demolition of churches, to the seizure of Bibles and the arrests of believers, are accompanied by strident anti-religious attacks on the church in the Marxist-Leninist government-controlled mass media.

'It is all part of Nicolae Ceausescu regime's aspirations to reshape the Romanian citizen into the "new man",' said an avid Romanian watcher. 'The regime's anti-religious campaign can only result in widening the gulf between the regime and its population, and in further tarnishing the regime's image in the West.

'It is partly as a result of such excesses that the regime has earned the unenviable reputation of being Eastern Europe's worst violator of human and religious rights, on a par with the Soviet Union—a consensus expressed in human rights assessments issued by Western governments and human rights organizations over the past few years.'

Another believer to suffer at the hands of Securitate is Dumitru Duduman, fifty-four, who was expelled from Romania in 1984 along with his wife Maria, and now lives in California. He told me that he was subjected to electric shocks, and even had nine of his ribs broken during beatings.

Duduman, who claims he has smuggled some three hundred thousand Bibles into the Soviet Union from his native Romania, said, 'After my arrest in August of 1980, I was put on the electric chair by the Secret Police to make me tell them where I was getting these Bibles. But I did not betray anyone. I never thought of betraying either my ministry or my brothers. I was willing to die first.

'On one occasion, I was strapped onto the electric chair and then they showed me the covered-up body of a friend whom they said had just died on the chair.'

Duduman also claimed he was subjected by Securitate to 'the water torture'.

'They used to have a very tiny room where you could not move, only stand, and they would put me in there barefoot and make me stand on some bars and then let cold water run over my feet,' said Duduman. 'After a while my legs became numb and I couldn't feel them any more.'

During 1981 and 1982, arrest and interrogation became a continuous way of life for him. In 1983, during another period of torture for his activities, he was hung by his waist and beaten three times.

'When I was their prisoner, the Secret Police did whatever they felt like,' he said. 'Often they would throw me on the floor and step on me with their boots. On one occasion, they cracked nine of my ribs. I have all the signs on my body to show what happened.'

Yet, despite everything, he and his wife continued to deliver Bibles, New Testaments and other Christian literature to the USSR. I asked Duduman why he took such risks in his work.

'There is as great a need for Bibles there as there is in Romania,' he replied. 'Because of so many problems and trials, hunger and lack of clothes in Romania and Russia, a lot of people are turning to God and therefore need the word of God.'

As I listened to him, I realized why Open Doors' couriers are taking such risks to take the word of God to these deprived Christians who deserve our help and our prayers. I could see that although Romanians are now materially among the poorest people in Eastern Europe, spiritually they may be the richest. So great is the revival sweeping across this land it is being called 'the South Korea of Europe'.

The most powerful statement of the trip came from a believer who tightly gripped his Bible and said, 'The deeper they drive in the nails, the deeper the roots of faith go down.'

We in the West can learn much from the Christians of Romania. They have truly been refined in the fire of suffering.

26

Return to Africa

The greater the power the more dangerous the abuse.
                                                    EDMUND BURKE

A small group of skeletal women, clad only in filthy brown
rags, made their way towards me in slow motion, their
bones thinly covered with skin, their faces reduced to
huge-eyed skulls. The scene in the continent of my birth
reminded me of photos I had seen from Auschwitz, but
instead this was the shocking reality of Ethiopia, circa
1985, where more than 300,000 had died of starvation in
the previous nine months. The desperately-sick mothers,
their matchstick children slung over their shoulders, began pleading with me to help them, mistaking me for a
doctor.

Within a short time the scene changed as a group of still
painfully thin, but now bright-eyed children with smiles
bigger than their faces, approached me. They had just
received food at this World Vision Feeding Centre at
Alamata in the north of the country, and began playfully
clasping my hands and arms and giggling as I took their
pictures. As I recorded their haunting images, a current of
air raised the dust that lay thick on the ground.

The ninety-minute flight from the comparative well-being of Addis Ababa to the primitive village people of Alamata was like going from my California home to the moon. The contrast was so vast.

Even as the de Havilland Twin Otter landed on the dusty strip, we could see that something was up. Four Russian helicopters, their blades scything through the hot air, were being loaded up at gunpoint with rag-clad people from local camps. They were being moved to another part of the country. Some were so terrified of the huge swinging rotors that they crawled on their hands and knees towards the helicopters.

It was only when I arrived at Alamata that I learned that my two Mission Aviation Fellowship flyers, John Hemstock and Andy Galloway, were involved in a life-or-death mission. If they failed, it could cost the lives of the very children who were clasping my hands and smiling brightly at me.

I learned of the imminent disaster from Dr Jim Owens, Alamata's resident doctor. This devoted man was near to tears as he spoke to me. 'We are facing a complete shutdown of the whole feeding centre tomorrow,' he said, the harrowing anguish showing all too clearly. 'That is, unless the pilots can get to us some desperately-needed vegetable oil that furnishes the calories to these starving people. You see, we mix it with grain, sugar and dried skimmed milk.'

The tragedy of the situation at Alamata, where nearly 10,000 were being fed, was brought starkly home to me by Linda McMillin of World Vision International.

'If the oil doesn't arrive I am sure that a good portion of them will die.' she said grimly. 'Those that don't die will certainly regress.'

As I walked around the feeding centre and watched mothers clasping their dying babies, begging me to help save their barely-alive offspring, I knew my eyes could not hold so much pain. What a responsibility the MAF flyers in Ethiopia had, I thought. For if they failed in *this* mission, thousands in this one camp alone could die within a short time.

But the pilots did not let them down! Just minutes before a curfew, which was strictly enforced by the Ethiopian Army controlling the airstrip, they again landed the Twin Otter. The vital oil supplies were unloaded and the death sentence about to be pronounced on 10,000 Ethiopians was lifted, at least temporarily.

'These pilots are definitely the unsung heroes of this whole relief operation in Ethiopia at this time,' said a relieved Dr Owens.

But there were thousands of other unsung heroes in this tragic land, as I discovered during my stay there. They were the Christians undergoing vicious persecution from the Marxist government of Lt Colonel Mengistu Haile Mariam.

'The government is closing many of the evangelical churches, so we are being forced to meet in secret,' a believer told me during a secret rendezvous. 'We already have a thriving underground church and it is growing at an incredible rate. We are praying that the government here continues with its persecution and closures because it is resulting in a stronger church and much more dedicated Christians.'

I discovered in Ethiopia that the Marxist Government, which seized power in 1974 from Haile Selassie, has been conducting, since 1977, a systematic effort to stamp out Christianity in the country.

While I was there in January 1985, some 1,800 of the 2,701 Kale Heywet churches had been closed. Kale Heywet, which means 'Word of Life', is the largest evangelical denomination in Ethiopia, comprising over half a million Christians. It originated from the work of the Sudan Interior Mission, with whom my parents had been associated in Nigeria.

My investigations revealed that secret Party directives

against religion from the Ethiopian Government written two years previously had come to light which set out a government blueprint for the abolition of religion from the country.

'This document proves claims made about the persecution of the Orthodox (church) in the past, and sets out a government blueprint for the total eradication of religion from society,' Michael Bordeaux, founder of Keston College, has explained. 'The document states the intention of confiscating possessions of the churches. The church will be subverted from within, through training of political cadres in Eastern Europe who would come to Ethiopia posing as priests. Special treatment (the Amharic word could be taken to mean liquidation) is reserved for those who stand out against this campaign.'

I discovered that hundreds, possibly thousands, of Ethiopian Christians had been imprisoned by the government, while overseas Christians who poured in millions of pounds of aid for the famine victims said nothing about the persecution because they feared this could prevent their relief work from continuing.

This present persecution had gone on consistently since 1977, and I spoke with Christians just recently released from prison after long spells. Their crime? 'Following Jesus Christ,' said one former prisoner. 'Like most Christians in Ethiopia, I was never charged formally, but it was made clear that I was being imprisoned because of my faith.'

An Ethiopian elder of an evangelical church said, 'It is too late for any government to wipe out the Ethiopian church. If Jesus had remained in the tomb, it would have been possible. Now the church is a reality through Christ's resurrection.'

Later investigations into the situation in Ethiopia in 1986 revealed that there could be as many as 7,000 Christians in prison in the country, according to information gathered by Open Doors couriers. The couriers said that this figure includes some 200 clergymen under arrest without trial in this Marxist country.

The research indicated that many of the imprisoned Christians have been jailed, not because of their Christian activities, but because of their actions in underground political movements, as well as with rebel movements.

But because of the crackdown, many of the Christians have organized themselves into cell groups and hold secret meetings for the celebration of the Lord's Supper and for baptism. And even the Orthodox youth have become involved in the renewal movement.

Bibles are said to be rationed in Ethiopia, even for the open churches.

'One case was reported to us of someone reading a Bible in public and being sentenced to imprisonment for several weeks,' said an Open Doors courier. 'In the western region, people are being arrested if they invite someone to attend a worship service. Reports are also reaching us that force is being used to prevent young people from visiting worship services.'

It appears that the Marxist government has also considered persecuting Muslims in the country, but has halted this for political reasons, wanting good relations with the Islamic countries. However, it doesn't worry too much about the so-called Christian nations being upset about Christians being persecuted. We don't appear to care!

On the plane home I reflected back on my life. I thought of the high price my parents had paid to bring the gospel to the 'dark continent', and how African Christians had played such a vital role in bringing me back to a full commitment to Christ. My parents' sacrifice had not been in vain!

I thought of my strange odyssey in Fleet Street, an experience that for years I had felt ashamed of. But now I could see that that too had all been in God's plan for my life. It had been a training ground for me to learn how to use those 'twenty-six lead soldiers'. I had learned the techniques of investigative journalism that were to prove invaluable as I tramped the world to gather the stories that I looked upon as 'Good News about Bad News'.

The Lord had clearly taught me that 'All things [do] work together for good to those that love God . . . .'

After I returned from Ethiopia, I read a letter which Corrie ten Boom received from her grandfather shortly before he died: 'I am living one day at a time. God's goodness is eternal and his faithfulness from generation to generation. I am so much enjoying the presence of the Lord and I wait for him. My suitcases are packed.'

I knew that soon I would be saying good-bye to Norma and the boys again. My bags would be packed and my next undercover mission would begin. My only regret is that there are so few who are willing to 'go' and bring love and encouragement to the forgotten heroes of the church.

I can only hope and pray that you, too, will get the vision to reach out to those who need our help and join the great battle; that those 'twenty-six lead soldiers' will also live in your life!

EPILOGUE

Imagine Albania

> I pray for the Albanian people and the leadership of Albania every day; that they may find God and also peace. I also pray for the underground church who are not afraid, and for all who suffer for their faith.
>
> MOTHER THERESA

> Even if we have to go without bread, we Albanians do not violate principles. We do not betray Marxist-Leninism.
>
> ENVER HOXHA

John Lennon voiced the desires of many people when, in his song 'Imagine', he envisaged a world with 'nothing to kill or die for and no religion too'. Well, a world without these ingredients doesn't exist, but one tiny nation in the Balkans, the People's Socialist Republic of Albania, has taken a giant step to rid itself of what Karl Marx called 'the opium of the people'.

I went with a group of eighteen British tourists in May 1986 to this mysterious land of Albania, which is ruled by the world's most Stalinist Communist party, to see if the fact that God has been abolished has brought the people the peace and happiness John Lennon dreamed about. Albania has certainly taken the teaching of Marxist-

237

Leninism to its logical conclusion and officially declared God dead. Since 1967, all churches and mosques have been closed for worship. Thousands of the Christian and Muslim leaders have been imprisoned or shot, and all vestiges of religion—it was seventy percent Muslim, the rest Orthodox and Catholic with just a handful of Protestants—have, on the surface, been brutally eradicated.

So there *is* still something to 'kill or die for' in Albania, but it seems, at first glance, that this beautiful mountainous country of nearly three million people, which shares a border with Yugoslavia in the north and Greece to the south, proves John Lennon's dream has come true—in part—with people living in harmony, and no religion interfering with their goal to be the world's purest socialistic society. As a special bonus, no one has to pay income tax and all medical and educational bills are paid by the state. They have even outlawed abortion, which is rampant in many of the so-called free nations of the West.

Albania is, however, a land that does not trust any other society except, perhaps, North Korea, and is on constant alert for invaders. Everywhere there are countless thousands of concrete 'pill-boxes'. Every valley, hill, beach, village, town and city has them.

Americans and Russians are not allowed into the country. I could understand why Americans were banned, but Russians?

'The reason is that they are revisionists,' I was told by one Albanian. 'We consider what they are doing in the world today as nothing but socialistic-imperialism.' In other words, they are too right wing for the Albanians!

But is Albania really the 'heaven on earth' that the aging leadership would like us to believe it is? The only way for me to learn the truth about the situation in this highly secretive society was to join a tour from Great Britain.

The official holiday brochure explained, 'As Albania is officially an atheistic state, Bibles and any other religious literature, whether or not for personal use, are not allowed to be brought into the country.'

Our group of eighteen flew from London to Titograd, Yugoslavia, and after a short stay there we were taken by bus to the Yugoslavian border post on an inlet of Lake Shkoder. After our passports were checked, we were given a short speech by the Yugoslavian guard that we 'must not try and bring back any Albania propaganda because it will be confiscated by us'. Then we had to carry our luggage across the fifty yards of no-man's land to the red-and-white border pike where a solemn-faced Albanian guard, dressed in an olive green uniform, heavy boots and with the obligatory red star on his cap, went through our passports and checked them against names and pictures on the multiple visa. A sign announced that we were about to enter the *Republika Popullore e Shqiperise* (Shqiperise being the 'Land of the Eagles').

As I looked at the guard's countenance, I could understand why, in 1810, British poet Lord Byron described Albania as 'a country rarely visited from the savage character of the natives'.

When he had finally completed his check, we were ushered with our luggage into a building dominated by a sign which quoted the Albanian strongman, Enver Hoxha (rhymes with dodger): 'Even if we have to go without bread, we Albanians do not violate principles. We do not betray Marxist-Leninism.' A picture of this austere man whose idol was Joseph Stalin gazed down at us as if to make sure we did nothing to 'corrupt' the 'world's first atheistic state'.

Each of us had to declare what we had brought with us and were subjected to a luggage search while David, our tour leader from Regent Holidays, looked anxiously on.

'On one occasion, I had a woman come in with religious tracts sewn inside her dress and later on in Shkoder she went out into the streets handing them out,' he told me. 'It caused quite a serious incident. The Albanians were very upset and watched us like hawks for the rest of the trip.'

That was nothing nearly as serious, however, as when New Zealander Reona Peterson was discovered, back in 1973, to have given a Gospel of John to a maid in her hotel. She was arrested and told she would be shot at dawn for her act. Fortunately, she was not executed but released and deported from Albania.

Nothing subversive was discovered in our group's luggage and we boarded the bus for the nearby town of Shkoder which houses the famous Atheist Museum. But instead of being taken to the museum, we were allowed to explore the town itself, where we saw the first bust of Stalin, an omnipresent sight in most Albanian cities.

'They have closed the Atheist Museum to foreigners because it caused too many arguments,' I was told when I enquired why we weren't going there.

But one earlier visitor to the museum, journalist Eric Newby, who later wrote about the experience in the *Sunday Express,* graphically described what it was like.

'We were shown "then" and "now" maps. The "then" ones were full of mosques and churches . . . before religion was officially abolished. The "now" maps—hey presto!—had no mosques or churches, most of them having been knocked down or blown up; but lots of schools.

'The visit was endless. The director, the first director of an atheist museum most of us had ever seen, laboriously described every exhibit in Albanian: confessional boxes, engravings of Inquisitors sending heretics up in smoke, photographs of mad-looking mullahs, priests engaged in what the caption described as "rock and rolli" with female parishioners, a hollowed-out Bible with a pistol in it, and so on. The interpreter laboriously turned all of it into English. When someone pointed out that the gun in the Bible was a dummy, the director said he hadn't noticed.'

There are Bibles in Albania; a few are hidden away in believers' homes, the others are in the churches that have been turned into museums. They are under glass in locked cases, so no one can actually read them. At one church-museum, we were shown the beautiful icons by a guide who chain-smoked and flicked his ash on the floor of the church.

Another guide, when asked about the mosques and churches, said, 'Some are now bars, others factories, schools, gymnasiums and museums.'

In Albania, a nation locked in a time warp, one is immediately struck by the lack of traffic. No one is allowed to own a car—the few that are seen on the streets are used by the party leadership. Most people walk. Outside the hotel, a traffic policeman frenetically blew his whistle at anything that moved, which was usually a Chinese-made bicycle or an ox-cart that rumbled slowly through the square.

The people were extremely friendly and many gazed in amazement at the strangely-dressed foreigners that had come to gaze in equal amazement at them as they went about their business. Young men affectionately walked arm-in-arm with each other, and young boys wearing their red Pioneer bandannas giggled as they posed for photographs.

I was surprised at the freedom we were given to talk and mix with the Albania people. Many wanted to practise their English and I will never forget walking into a little coffee shop and being immediately approached by a smiling young man who asked me if I would join him for coffee. He insisted on paying for it and began talking to me in faltering English.

On another occasion, I was able to ask an Albanian why religion had been banned in the country.

'Because it was brought here by the invaders,' he said firmly. 'For instance, the Turks brought Islam, the Greeks brought the Orthodox religion and the Italians brought the Catholic faith. We consider that religion was introduced by outsiders, so we don't need it.'

'But,' I countered, 'wasn't Karl Marx a foreigner, too?' My friend looked embarrassed and sipped his drink.

I asked an Albanian woman if atheism was taught to the children in the schools. 'Of course! We try and show why religion was just a superstition. If I asked God for something now, would he give it to me?' she snapped. 'Of course he wouldn't, because he doesn't exist!' The children are also encouraged to inform on their parents and turn them over to the authorities if they suspect they are 'disruptive to the Party'.

I then asked if there were any Christians left in the country?

'Maybe a few old people who pray in their homes, but that's all. There are definitely no young people who believe. They have never been taught about religion and therefore do not accept it or follow it.'

My investigations revealed, however, that all the teaching and brutality directed against 'the people of the book', has failed to wipe out the God-shaped void in the Albanian people, whose most famous supporter is Mother Theresa of Calcutta, herself an Albanian.

'I pray for the Albanian people and the leadership of Albania every day; that they may find God and also peace. I also pray for the underground church who are not afraid, and for all who suffer for their faith,' the Nobel Peace Prize-winner once said.

There are scores of horror stories of Christians in Albania who have paid the ultimate penalty for their faith. The Albania Catholic Information Centre, California, has reported that the persecution still continues. In May 1980, Jesuit Father Ndoc Luli disappeared after secretly baptizing two children of his nephew's wife. At the time of the Communist takeover in 1944, he had been arrested and sentenced to fifteen years of hard labour in prison. Having served the full term, he was released and confined to his native village near Shkoder. A year later, due to frail health, he was allowed to join his family in Mail Jushit, a village nearby. He was forced to work in the state-owned Agricultural Co-operative as a labourer in the stockyards, and he was also prohibited from performing priestly duties.

When asked to baptize the new-born twins in May 1980, he hesitated for some time. He knew that his fellow priest, Shtjefen Kurti, had been executed in 1972 for baptizing a baby boy in a labour camp. Eventually, he agreed to perform the rite. The parents and a few relatives were present at the secret ceremony, but unfortunately the news leaked out to *Sigurimi,* Albania's hated secret police, and he was arrested and interrogated, along with his nephew's wife, and brought to a public trial.

After much humiliation, his nephew's wife was sentenced to eight years in prison at hard labour, while the priest's ambiguous sentence was 'life until death'.

'His family have been unable to locate him ever since. His fate is unknown, although many believe his life came to an end at the bottom of a mine pit, victim of the dreaded *Sigurimi,'* said a spokesman for the Albania Catholic Information Centre.

Jak Gardin, a Jesuit priest now living in Italy, who was a fellow prisoner with Father Luli in various Albanian prisons and labour camps, commented, 'The best I can say about Father Luli is that I felt privileged to have carried with him the chains of pain and persecution for our faith. I didn't realize that the crown of martyrdom would rest over his head thirty years later. Today, at this time, he is a martyr of Christ and with this, all is said.'

Father Gardin spent ten years in Albanian prisons and labour camps. In his diary he records the sacrifices made by priests and other Christians for the well-being of their fellow prisoners, many of whom were non-Catholics. When their fellow prisoners had their rations of bread and soup withheld for being unable to meet the heavy work quotas, he and other priests would happily share and even give all their daily rations to those being punished. 'It was a sacrifice which nourished our strength and filled our hearts with contentment,' he wrote.

In Durres, I stood in the lions' cage of the amphitheatre where, in Roman times, the lions were released to kill and devour the Christians in front of a cheering crowd. I could feel the irony of the situation in present-day Albania.

The hatred of all religion is further shown by the fact that in September 1975, a new law was made prohibiting religious names for the newborn. In June, 1977, a new Albanian penal code was issued, clause 55 of which lays down the penalties to be exacted for religious activity. It states that 'religious propaganda, and also the production, distribution or storage of literature of this kind' will be punished with imprisonment for between three and ten years. In a time of war or if the offences are deemed to be serious, imprisonment is for not less than ten years and the death penalty can be imposed.

When the new constitution was introduced in 1967, this resulted in prayer in schools not only being outlawed overnight, but all prayer anywhere being banned. Hoxha ordered a final attack to wipe out the church and all religious activity. In his notorious speech of February 6, 1967, he urged Albanian youth to fight 'religious superstitions' with all their vigour. A strong anti-religious campaign followed. Churches and mosques everywhere were burned or converted for other uses; priests and bishops were publicly beaten, arrested and sent to prisons and labour camps for 're-education'. By the end of the year, 2,200 churches, mosques, chapels and other religious buildings were vandalized and closed. Even the crosses on grave stones were removed.

There was only one messiah to be allowed in Albania, Enver Hoxha. He became the only way and the truth and the life for the people. And to remind them of this, his sayings were put on every public building and his name inscribed on every hill and mountain.

Enver Hoxha was a very charming man and a fluent

orator. He was also deeply suspicious and quite ruthless. 'His path to power and in power was strewn with the corpses of his enemies,' said John Halliday writing in *The Guardian*. They were also strewn with the corpses of his former friends. While I was in Albania, I was told that the last major killing he was involved in was that of Mehmet Shehu, who had been Albanian Prime Minister for more than twenty-five years. On December 18, 1981, they had met for dinner to discuss a difference that had arisen between them. Shehu felt it was about time that Albania abandoned its unique policy of total isolation from the world and begin to re-enter it. Hoxha was said to have become so angry that he drew his pistol and shot the Prime Minister dead on the spot. *Radio Tirana* announced then that Shehu 'in a moment of nervous crisis' had committed suicide.

To try and understand the situation in Albania, I talked to several Albanian emigrants, one being Father Andrew, an Albanian-born priest now teaching philosophy and theology in America. He described the regime in his homeland in strong terms: 'If Joseph Stalin and Ayatollah Komeini were united together, this would explain what has happened in Albania.'

On April 11, 1985, Hoxha died at the age of seventy-six, after ruling the country with an iron fist for forty years. He was the longest-lasting non-hereditary leader in the world, having been in power consistently since the country's liberation in November 1944. He had out-distanced Stalin, Mao and even Tito.

'Many of the people we saw in Tirana, the capital, were crying,' said an eye-witness in Albania at the time of Hoxha's death. 'Some were rolling on the floor with shock. One man told me as he wept, "Enver Hoxha has made this country what it is and also made me what I am." The Albanian people were so indoctrinated that they really did love him. They believed him to be their messiah.'

Hoxha has been succeeded by Ramiz Alia. The Soviets sent their condolences to Tirana, but they were immediately returned to Moscow.

'The Soviet Union is a threat to the freedom of our people,' said the Albanian embassy in Vienna, commenting on the new leadership's first and telling act. So would things ease now for believers in the country?

A recent report in a Czech Catholic journal reports that Ramiz Alia, the General Secretary of the Communist Party of Albania, has declared that people should not be imprisoned, or otherwise punished, for praying at home. If this information is correct, it will be an extremely significant development since Albania was officially proclaimed atheistic in 1967, and has severely punished religious worship in private homes in the past.

But this does not appear to be borne out by the news that Jesuit Priest Pjeter Meshkalla, an outspoken critic of the Albanian government's anti-religious laws and practices, has been arrested again for conducting religious services.

'According to information from recent Albanian refugees, Father Meshkalla was arrested while celebrating Christmas Mass in a private home near Shkoder,' said a spokesman for the Albania Catholic Information Centre.

He has served a total of thirty-four years in Albanian prisons and labour camps and is eighty years old.

'This news proves that the crackdown is still in force, and also that there are house groups meeting for prayer and worship in Albania,' said a spokesman for Open Doors.

'Alia was the man behind the rewriting of the new constitution that introduced the "world's first atheistic state", so don't expect too many changes in Albania. But, on the other hand, Albania could go like China after the death of Mao. Too many people there are disillusioned and will go and search for another truth. We all hope they will, in the end, find the whole truth, the real truth.'

I asked an Albanian if the country would now open up. 'Certainly not,' I was told. 'We will continue the same policies under the leadership of Ramiz Alia. He was a close friend and ally of Enver Hoxha.'

That is bad news for the well-over 20,000 political and religious prisoners in the land *The Guardian* described as 'The Little Country With The Big Gulag'. The prisoners include thousands of priests and others who refused to bow to Hoxha's version of Socialist purity.

To put the whole situation in Albania in perspective, I asked a Marxist travelling with us to explain why Marxism did not consider the well-being of the individual, something which Christianity taught.

'The good of the individual is not considered,' he said chillingly. 'That is why Christianity is the total enemy of Marxism and should not be tolerated.'

It was obvious to me that John Lennon's dream has not come true in Albania. But the country has some important lessons to teach us. Freedom does not exist there, but what we call freedom in the West has turned to licence. When millions of unborn are 'terminated', when divorce has reached epidemic proportions, and drug addiction has become a major problem, we have to wonder what impact 'religion' is having in the West.

The fact is that 'religion' is having no impact at all. It is a personal relationship with Jesus Christ that is important, not following man-made institutions.

In Albania, the media are totally controlled by the government. We in the West have a mass media that are supposed to be free. But what do we do with them? We produce *junk!* We have many papers totally dedicated to titillating, not uplifting, their millions of readers. 'Never let the facts interfere with a good story,' one Fleet Street reporter was said to have declared. But even Fleet Street cannot match the fiction of the French press.

Henry Porter, in his book, *Lies, Damned Lies* (Coronet Books) wrote:

A French newspaper once conducted a survey of the way in which the French press presented the British Royal Family, and came up with the following set of statistics. Between 1958 and 1972 the Queen was pregnant ninety-two times, had 149 accidents and nine miscarriages and took the pill eleven times. She abdicated sixty-three times and was on the point of breaking up with Prince Philip seventy-three times. She was said to be fed up 112 times and on the verge of a nervous breakdown thirty-two times. She had forty-three unhappy nights, twenty-seven nightmares, and her life was threatened twenty-nine times. She was rude to the Queen of Persia eleven times, to Princess Grace of Monaco six times and to Queen Fabiola only twice; and she expelled Lord Snowdon from Court 151 times.

My favourite piece of press fiction was headlined in an American tabloid, 'Adolf Hitler lives; led Falklands invasion.'

Our television networks don't fare much better, producing moronic 'soaps' because that is what they assume the public wants. The film industry glorifies violence on an unparalleled 'Rambo' scale. Our media leaders often set no example with their own personal lives. In many cases, it's the blind leading the blind . . . into the ditches.

Christians around the world appear to be largely deaf to the cries of their suffering brothers and sisters. I asked Brother Andrew to have a final word in this book on how we can unplug our ears to the pleas for help from the suffering church.

'First, you *must* be prepared to hear the cries of those who are suffering,' he said. 'Did you know that sixty-six percent of the body of Christ now live in restricted countries and suffer persecution from antagonistic regimes, both political and religious? You will hear those cries by reading material put out by ministries like Open Doors.

'And what can you do? Our first and foremost need is for people to *pray*. This is a spiritual battle which must be fought with spiritual weapons and warfare. We need you to join the battle with us, to break down the spiritual strongholds of darkness, so that the believers in the suffering church will be strengthened, comforted and enabled to live victorious lives in the midst of their suffering.

'Then you will also hear the cries of those who are suffering by going to those countries and meeting those incredible believers.

'"But I can't go to Russia, Iran or Cuba," you may say. Why not? Don't you believe that God will protect you? If you know he is calling you, and if you take that step of faith, you will not only give, but you will receive from Christians of a calibre you have never met before. And they will be so grateful that you took the trouble to leave your comfortable country to help them.

'Every place I have gone in the world, the believers have said, "Andrew even if you hadn't brought Bibles, your visit would have been worth while because now we know we are not forgotten." Will you show them that they are not forgotten?

'You can also give. You can support ministries like Open Doors that provide Bibles and other much-needed help and encouragement to the suffering church.

'The question is, are you willing to feel their pain and suffering and do something about it? Only then, I believe, will God turn your country once again into a God-fearing nation.'

I hope that these preceding 'twenty-six lead soldiers' will challenge you to march with us. It's a long march . . . but you could help change history. Or are you going to allow Karl Marx's dream to come true?

More information concerning the ministry of Open Doors
with Brother Andrew can be obtained from the following
addresses:

P.O. Box 47
3850AA Ermelo
HOLLAND

P.O. Box 6
Standlake
Witney
Oxon
OX8 7SP
ENGLAND

P.O. Box 53
Seaforth
NSW 2092
AUSTRALIA

P.O. Box 6123
Auckland 1
NEW ZEALAND

P.O. Box 990099
Kibler Park
2053 Johannesburg
SOUTH AFRICA

P.O. Box 27001
Santa Ana
CA 92799
UNITED STATES OF AMERICA